STRIPPED DOWN

13 KEYS TO UNLOCKING INTIMACY IN YOUR MARRIAGE

Tony & Alisa DiLorenzo

PRAISE FOR STRIPPED DOWN

"As a life coach I see many people who have created strategies for business success. But those same people frequently have no plan for success in the most important areas of life. In *Stripped Down*, Tony and Alisa share clear systems and processes for being as intentional about success in your marriage as you would expect in your business. With no plan in place, your business – or your marriage – will likely fail. Don't take that chance."

–Dan Miller, author, *48 Days to the Work You Love*, and Life Coach, 48days.com

"Misunderstandings abound on the subject of intimacy. The DiLorenzo's "strip down" those false assumptions and look at what intimacy truly is in the context of a marriage relationship! A "must read" for all couples!"

–Ken and Pam Ingold, Family Pastors, The Church at Rancho Bernardo

"If you think you know what intimacy in marriage means, think again. Tony and Alisa DiLorenzo unwrap not just one, but 13 simple keys to inspire soul-bonding, gratifying intimacy in six different areas of your marriage. Don't just read this book – do what they say!"

–Gina Parris, author, *The Romance Rescue*
How to Have Really Great Sex When You're NOT in the Mood.

"*Stripped Down* is such a relevant and necessary read for so many couples. This book takes a very practical approach to connecting with your spouse in a deep, fulfilling way. I applaud Tony and Alisa's openness and honesty about intimacy; it's a refreshing reminder that we're never beyond our vows."

–Derek Sisterhen, Financial Coach and author of
Get Naked: Stripping Down to Money & Marriage

"Tony & Alisa are trusted authorities on the topic of intimacy. *Stripped Down* showcases their down-to-earth style in teaching all of us how we can get (and give) more in this vital area of our marriages. I highly recommend this book for any couple interested in making their marriage extraordinary!"

–Dustin Riechmann, EngagedMarriage.com

"Looking to dive in to the world of intimacy in marriage? *Stripped Down* is a great way to do so. Not only is the whole book about intimacy and its place in marriage, it goes even deeper by breaking it down into 6 different types and explores each one. Plus, Tony and Alisa add their "his" and "hers" takes to the process and make it easy for everyone to improve their marriage right away."

–Corey Allen, Ph.D., Simple Marriage, SimpleMarriage.com

"*Stripped Down* is not only a fantastic story but a fun practical tool for every marriage! If you are ready to take your marriage to the "NEXT LEVEL" then apply the principles so clearly detailed in Tony and Alisa's book."

–Jay & Laura Laffoon, authors, *He Said. She Said, Woo Her Woo Him, I Did! Growing Intimacy For a Lifetime Together*, www.celebratenet.com.

"*Stripped Down* is full of practical advice on the most important human relationship we have on Earth. Tony & Alisa are the real deal! Their open and authentic approach to the topic of intimacy in marriage is refreshing in a world that blushes at the thought of having conversations around this gift that God has given to married couples. We believe this is a conversation that all married couples should have and that this book is a great place to start."

–Cliff & Stephanie Ravenscraft,
Hosts of Family From The Heart at FamilyFromTheHeart.com

"If you thought the Honeymoon couldn't last...Think Again! With uncharacteristic candor and an engaging conversational style, the DiLorenzos reveal the secret to an Intimacy in marriage that goes the distance! *Stripped Down* is a must read for Marriage!"

–Harry Kuehl, Senior Pastor, The Church at Rancho Bernardo

STRIPPED DOWN

13 KEYS TO

UNLOCKING

INTIMACY

IN YOUR

MARRIAGE

Tony & Alisa DiLorenzo

PastDue: Press

Past Due: Press
527 Keisler Drive, Suite 204
Cary, NC 27518

PastDuePress.com

To purchase more copies or to inquire about Tony and Alisa visit
www.OneExtraordinaryMarriage.com.

ISBN: 978-0-9825465-2-9

Art Direction, Design, Production, Consultation: Studio 6 Sense, www.studio6sense.com

Editorial assistance provided by Word Weaver 4 U, www.wordweaver4u.com

Stripped Down: 13 Keys to Unlocking Intimacy in Your Marriage / Tony and Alisa DiLorenzo

ISBN: 978-0-9825465-2-9

1. Marriage 2. Intimacy

Printed in the United States of America by PastDuePress.com

DEDICATION

*To our Lord and Savior, Jesus Christ, for the strength and courage
to do this "thing" called marriage, every day.*

CONTENTS

ACKNOWLEDGMENTS

This book has literally been a labor of love. We had no idea what we were getting ourselves into when we decided to write a book together! It has been a fascinating journey through drafts and revisions, late nights in front of the computer and countless discussions on the topics inside. This book would not have been possible without the assistance and encouragement of many.

To those of you in the Intimacy Ignited small group: You were our first accountability partners. You listened as we shared the ups and downs of our 60 Days of Sex. Your encouragement, laughter and hugs helped us through that "experiment" and we are indebted to you for your support.

Thank you to the Marriage Ministry at The Church at Rancho Bernardo. Your invitation to speak at the 2009 Marriage Conference allowed us to share this story with our first large audience. We didn't know at the time how many people this story would touch or how it would change lives.

To those of you who read this book, gave us your feedback and helped us through this process, there are not words enough to say how appreciative we are of your time and effort.

To our followers on OneExtraordinaryMarriage.com, Twitter and Facebook: You have shown us that there is a need for this message, that people desire extraordinary marriages. Thank you for being a part of the ONE community.

We learned how to be married and stay married from our parents, Carmen and Vincie DiLorenzo and Lu and Beth Torres. Both couples were married within two months of each other in 1972 and are still going strong. Thank you for the life lessons in commitment, perseverance and love.

To our children, who have changed the way that we look at the world. It is because of you that we have such a desire to have a strong marriage. The two of you put up with imperfect parents and love us anyway!

To my husband, who puts up with a lot and still manages to keep a smile on his face. I love growing older with you, knowing that the best is yet to come.

To my wife: I never imagined a marriage this amazing after so many years. Your willingness to ride this roller coaster we call marriage together has inspired me to give everything I have to you. I wouldn't want it any other way.

FOREWORD

Remember back to your wedding day. We're not talking about just the ceremony and reception. We want you to remember how you felt. Think back to when you were gazing into the eyes of your intended spouse and how happy you were. Your marriage was going to last forever. You were sure of that much.

Why were you so sure? Because this man or woman made you feel so special. Maybe your new husband was the most romantic guy you had ever met. Maybe your new wife was one of the most incredible people you had ever met. Both of you knew that this was a marriage that would work. Your life would always remain as magical as it was in the very beginning.

You spent the first few months settling in as a married couple. Perhaps you couldn't keep your hands off of each other and made those around you roll their eyes with envy as they watched the two of you. But you didn't care – you were in love!

And then… reality sets in. You start to notice little things about your true love that drive you crazy. You think you can deal with it, and maybe you can – for awhile. But then, you start to pull away just a little bit. You still love your spouse, but it's just not the same.

You start to take each other for granted. After all, you're married. That's part of married life, isn't it? Then you wake up one morning and look over at your love. You wonder what happened to that fire, that amazing desire that couldn't be controlled. Why don't you feel like you did on your honeymoon?

Work, household obligations, child rearing (if you have kids), being together 24/7, and your many other activities begin to sap the energy and romance from your marriage. You don't spend quality time with your spouse any longer as you start taking each other for granted.

It does not have to be this way. There are many relationships where romance is alive and well. Open up your local paper and look for the anniversary announcements.

It can actually be very motivating to see couples celebrating their 25th, 30th, even 50th wedding anniversaries.

In case you think this is a trivial subject, please know intimacy is important to the health and well being of your relationship. Being intimate in your marriage is celebrating your partner every day for who they are.

If the intimacy dies, one or both people in the marriage will begin to feel unappreciated. For many, this can be the beginning of the end of the relationship, or perhaps the beginning of an affair.

Is it just a part of life? Do you let that fire die into just a smoldering pile of ashes? You don't have to! In fact, there is no reason at all why you can't get back what you had when you were newlyweds. It just takes a little effort.

There are millions of married couples out there who know what it takes to stay in love and keep their marriages fresh and new. Want to know their secrets? No problem!

Keeping intimacy alive and well in your marriage can be achieved, but it does take work. Anything in life that is truly good and satisfying takes work. However, **the rewards are HUGE**, so make the effort! As you go through this workbook, make sure to read it with your spouse. Complete the questions and exercises so that the two of you can strengthen and build your marriage together. We're here to help you find the fire, passion, and romance in your marriage, but it is up to you to take the first step. Let's get started.

OUR STORY

Before we start working on your marriage, you might want to know a little about ours.

Flashback to October 1996: I (Tony) stood waiting. I'd been here much longer than I'd expected. A crowd waited in front of me, while my best man stood at my side. Alisa, my soon-to-be wife, was nowhere to be found. I looked at the pastor with an awkward smile, wondering what was happening. Our wedding was supposed to start ten minutes ago. My dad had just stood up and said, "I don't think she's coming." Where was she? Was I getting jilted at the altar?

At last, over the horizon, my beautiful bride came into view in a horse-drawn carriage. The guests cheered as relief washed over me. Alisa and I said "I do" and embarked upon our happily ever after. We had an awesome wedding and an amazing honeymoon, with the exception of the diesel leak when we were snorkeling, but that's another story. If this was married life, we were in heaven. Little did we know there's a reason it's called a honeymoon phase.

It didn't take long to discover that this marriage thing was harder than it looked. Things that weren't a big deal when we were dating didn't go away once we got married. She was not opposed to clutter or "little" messes, our communication styles were vastly different, and when we got into arguments I wanted to talk through the issue while she shut down and didn't want to talk at all. As the years began to pass, we experienced the highs and lows a marriage inevitably brings. Long work days meant we barely saw each other, and we began growing apart. For a time, I filled the void with alcohol, drugs, and pornography.

Four years into our marriage, I hiked the Pacific Crest Trail from Mexico to Canada. Over the course of four months, Alisa and I went days or even weeks without contact. When I returned home, we could no longer ignore the gaping distance between us. Alisa and I were so far apart that it hurt. The intimate conversations of our courtship

For this reason a man will leave his father and mother and be united to his wife, and they will become one flesh.

—Genesis 2:24

had given way to yelling and screaming, and tears poured down both our faces as we considered getting a divorce.

Somehow, we managed to make things work, and our son was born in 2002. But when Alisa suffered a miscarriage a couple of years later, the decline toward divorce began again. Alisa fell into an intense depression, and while I had overcome my addictions, I admit I wasn't much help. When our daughter was born a year after the miscarriage, we were so busy being parents that we neglected our roles as husband and wife.

Something had to change. God had more in store for our lives, and I knew it. What I didn't know was how to climb out of the hole we were in.

Eleven years into our marriage, Alisa and I needed a way to reconnect. As we prepared to lead a small group on intimacy I knew we needed to do something more for ourselves and our relationship. Our marriage was all about routine. We had lost the spark we'd had in the beginning of our marriage and were just going through the motions, each and every day. One night, after watching an online news segment discussing intimacy, I threw this idea out to Alisa: "Let's make love every night for the next two months."

"No."

The answer flew so fast out of Alisa's mouth that I was taken aback. I hoped we could at least talk about it, but for her, it wasn't up for discussion. Truth be told, I was bummed and a little relieved at the same time – bummed because I thought this could have been the way to recharge our marriage, and have a lot of sex to boot, and relieved because, well, eight weeks of sex is *a lot* of sex. Alisa began getting ready for bed, and to my surprise, I heard a faint "I'll think about it." But I wasn't getting my hopes up. So the next day, when Alisa said, "Let's do it, Tony," I actually responded, "Do what?"

Alisa looked at me from across the room. "Let's make love every night for the next eight weeks." I couldn't believe she was willing to give it a shot. My mind started racing. *I'm going to get sex every night for two months. What if I get tired? Will the kids stay in their bedrooms? What on earth are we doing?*

We left it in God's hands, and while it didn't happen every night during those eight weeks, we were intimate 40 times (more than we had done in the previous two years), learning more about intimacy than we ever dreamed – and not just physical intimacy. We began to connect in a way that we hadn't in more than a decade.

We are a normal couple who set out on an extraordinary path to rediscover intimacy in our marriage. Our "60 Days of Sex" and the ensuing years have taught us so much that we just can't keep it to ourselves. You hold in your hands the keys to bringing back passion, love, and intimacy in your marriage.

If you picked up this book, you clearly have a desire to deepen the bonds of your relationship. But desire alone will not change a marriage. For the next 60 days, make a commitment to put the 13 Keys to work. Take a leap of faith – journal your experiences, share your discoveries, and see the changes that 60 days of intimacy will make.

—Tony and Alisa DiLorenzo

Growth means change and change involves risk, stepping from the known to the unknown.

—Shinn George

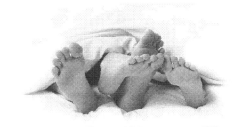

WHAT IS INTIMACY?

1

Easy...it's sex, right? Yes and no.

Intimacy is closeness with another person. Sex is often the first thing we think of when we hear the word intimacy. Most people don't realize that there are other forms of intimacy that allow us to have an extraordinary marriage. The six forms of intimacy are:

Emotional Intimacy is closeness created through sharing our feelings, thoughts and desires. You have to be honest, first with yourself, regarding your feelings before you can share them with your spouse.

Intellectual Intimacy involves a mutual understanding about the important areas or issues in your marriage. Perhaps you want to set goals for the next year, you want to make a budget, you want to raise your children with certain values, and all of these involve discussion without fear of repercussion. Intellectual intimacy means you have made your marriage a safe place for discussion. **Visit www.oneextraordinarymarriage .com/resources** to download the goal setting worksheet.

Spiritual Intimacy is shared religious beliefs and observed religious practices. This can be as simple as praying together (although that's not always easy), going to church together or discussing spiritual issues as a couple. Ultimately your life experiences, within the foundation of your shared faith, will create and deepen your spiritual intimacy.

Recreational Intimacy is being active together. Find things you both like to do and do them with each other. Take a walk together, make dinner, go to a museum, hike a mountain – do something with your spouse that allows you to actively spend time together.

Financial Intimacy is the sharing of your financial situation. Financial intimacy comes with developing a plan for your finances and being able to have open and honest communication with your spouse regarding money matters.

Physical Intimacy is loving touch. Be it holding hands, a hug, a kiss or making love, we humans were designed to want to be touched. Touch can communicate acceptance and love, a closeness that only the two of you have based on your shared experiences.

These six intimacies are vital to a successful marriage, a marriage based on safety and trust. Our 13 Keys explore each of these to help you have a marriage that is extraordinary. Each Key in this book is tagged with a specific intimacy from the list above. This will help you to recognize the form of intimacy being discussed. As you read each chapter, take notes to help you realize where your relationship is overflowing with intimacy and where it needs some filling. It can seem daunting at times to even start working on your marriage, but take the first step.

Alisa and I have been married many years, and can tell you that it's awesome when the two of you are on the same page. The intimacy we have today has grown from when we first got married, had our kids, and went through the difficult times. The time and effort we have put forth has balanced out the six forms of intimacy and helped us to understand each other better. Ultimately, we are happier, more passionate, and more in love than ever.

Creating intimacy involves:

- consistent attention to one another and the relationship itself
- respect for each other, and for the relationship in particular
- regular, healthy verbal communication
- regular expressions of caring and tenderness
- honesty
- understanding
- encouragement

Questions

1. Is intimacy a necessity or a luxury in today's world?

2. In your opinion, what is the greatest myth about intimacy?

3. What in your marriage can you focus on for the next two months that will strengthen your foundation?

4. What do you do when you are intimate that really makes you feel good?

5. Do you have any intimacy needs (emotional, intellectual, spiritual, recreational, financial, and physical) in your marriage that aren't being met right now?

Many marriages would be better if the husband and the wife clearly understood that they are on the same side.

—Zig Ziglar

FROM THE TOP DOWN
SPIRITUAL INTIMACY

2

One of the greatest threats to intimacy in marriage is living life upside down. There is no shortage of people, things, and activities that compete to be number one in our lives. Maybe you define yourself primarily by your job, or your net worth, or your children. Maybe it's more important to you to have the status symbols of success or accomplishment. Maybe you feel a sense that there is, or should be, something more. Maybe your priorities are out of whack.

Our early years of marriage were way out of whack. We didn't have our priorities in order, and this led to disagreements, resentment and a lack of intimacy in our marriage. We lived trying to satisfy ourselves with material things, other relationships, and the pursuit of money. None of these were working, and as the years passed we found ourselves falling farther and farther apart from each other.

Alisa says...

In 2000, almost four years into our marriage, Tony embarked on an adventure that would forever change our lives: he hiked the Pacific Crest Trail from Mexico to Canada. While he was out there, with way to much time on his hands, he met "Arkansas" Dave. As Tony and Dave hiked they had many conversations about life and the pursuit of happiness. One evening while they were getting camp set up in Oregon, Dave handed Tony a Bible. It was there that Tony began his search for the Creator of the Universe, unbeknownst to me.

I was going through my own transformation at home, time away from Tony and a break-in at our apartment having changed my life forever. My search for God was happening, too.

After four and a half months apart, our reunion was bittersweet. We had both grown, but we had also grown apart. Tough times and the discussion of divorce entered our house for the first and only time. We were at our lowest point in our marriage. The pain, resentment, and lack of communication brought us to our knees. For the first time, we took a step of faith and went to church together.

This was to be a life-changing decision. We began to find the answers we were looking for, and the emptiness we had begun to feel faded as our relationship with Christ began to grow. We committed our lives to Christ in 2001, but still didn't really know what it meant to live a Christ-centered life. Over the next four years, we began growing in Christ and learning how to have Christ at the center of our marriage. Our marriage was truly *reborn* in 2004 following the loss of our son, Andrew, through miscarriage. This crisis could have easily destroyed our marriage, and as I dealt with my depression this wasn't an unlikely scenario. We were struggling with how to relate to one another, how to move forward, how to make our marriage work. We realized that we weren't going to be able to do this alone, and turned to God for help. He is the reason that our marriage is where it is today.

We believe that Jesus Christ is our Lord and Savior. He is the foundation of our marriage, and without Him we wouldn't have the extraordinary marriage we have today. The 13 Keys are based on this understanding. Does this mean that if you do not know or follow Christ, you cannot benefit from this book? **Absolutely not.** The principles in this book can be applied to all marriages, regardless of your faith background. If there is something missing in your marriage, we hope you and your spouse will begin to search for the answers.

Keeping our priorities in order isn't always easy, but it is essential if you want your marriage to be the best it can be. Placing God at the center of your relationship creates the most solid marital foundation. Once you have God as the anchor of your marriage, your spouse comes next in terms of priority. That creates a united front for your next

When we put God first, all other things fall into their proper place or drop out of our lives.

—Ezra Taft Benson

priority: your kids. Your career comes in at number four. Maintaining this order allows you to keep your focus on the things that matter in the order that they matter. When you mix up your priorities, you venture into dangerous territory.

Take 10-15 minutes to honestly evaluate where you stand with your priorities. Pull out your daily planner and go back over the last two weeks to see how you are spending your time. Do your actions match what you believe your priorities should be?

Here's how they should be listed:

- God
- Spouse
- Family
- Work
- Other activities

I'm going to guess that your actions and what you say is important don't completely match up. How do I know this? Because mine don't always match up either. It's human nature. I can often be seen sitting on Facebook or checking emails. I'll stop playing with my kids to take a phone call. I often try and do one more work "thing" before spending time with Tony. There are so many demands on our time that we often lose sight of the way our lives should be ordered. What happens then? Our lives fall completely out of balance, and the things we should focus on – those whom we love – are relegated to the bottom of the list. Here's the sad part: <u>they know it</u>.

Instead of simply reacting, sometimes we need to put more thought into our moment-to-moment existence. That's how I determine whether my priorities are off track. Do I really need to check my email again? Can I let a call go to voicemail? Is it critical that I wash dishes at this very minute? Probably not.

I am guilty of choosing work and little things on my "To Do" list over spending time with my husband and children. I often find myself thinking I would have more time with them if I could just get one more thing on my "To Do" list done. The reality is that my "To Do" list is never completely done, and whether I want to admit it or not, these family relationships require that I be engaged in order to thrive.

Consider the alternatives.

Would my time be better spent engaging in the important relationships in my life? Do I need to stop what I am doing and spend more time in prayer, more time with my

Bible? Have I told my husband lately how much I appreciate him? Do my kids get my full attention, or do they get the leftovers? Does work hold the proper place in my life?

I have found that when I spend more time in prayer, truly connecting with God instead of just going through the motions, my life seems a little bit easier. This isn't to say that I don't have problems, but rather that I am better able to handle the problems. And when I let Tony know how much I appreciate all that he does for me and for our family, he's more willing to help out around the house and with the kids. My acknowledgment of his efforts makes him more willing to lighten my load. It's so easy to see that when I put the proper attention on our kids, they are more cooperative and there are fewer behavioral problems. Knowing all of this, you would think I would get it right, and yet I still find myself demonstrating a nature that's more selfish than serving and ending up stuck with the consequences of those decisions.

Mixing up any of your priorities has detrimental effects on all your priorities. If your relationship with God is not right, your other relationships will not be right either. If your husband (or wife) does not hold second place, there will be imbalance in your marriage. When people focus on their kids to the neglect of their spouses, the very structure of their family life becomes unstable. Being parents without remembering that you are also husband and wife has undone many a marriage. And work... yes, we need to be able to pay our bills and put a roof over our heads, but career, money, and the pursuit of material success cannot become your god. You may have a very important and worthy job, but it is easy to see that your marriage will suffer when you become married to your career.

One woman we know was quite open about the reason her first marriage had failed. Her children were "her life." Everything was about the kids; they came first, no matter what. There was nothing her husband could do to earn his place above the children, and ultimately this marriage failed. I experienced a similar situation with my work. When I first started my own business, it was easy to get wrapped up in the details, to think that I had to take care of everything "right now." The impact this had on my marriage and children was not worth the price. They began to resent what I was doing, and I had to make changes to balance what I wanted and what was beneficial for the family. Nothing is worth the sacrifice of your marriage and your relationship with your children.

You are the only one who knows what is truly in your heart in terms of the focal points of your life. And you are the only one who can reprioritize the elements of your life

Attempt something so impossible that unless God is in it, it's doomed to failure.

—John Haggai

if necessary. You must begin to take baby steps to make the changes that are required to put your life in balance. I remind myself daily, sometimes in the moment, that my priorities are God first, then Tony, then the kids, then work, and finally, everything else. When Tony reminds me that I'm off-balance, I acknowledge that he's right and make the effort to stop what I'm doing and get back to what I need to be doing. I try to say no to those things that are going to upset the order.

Is it easy? No. Is it something I have to continue to work on every day? Absolutely. But work on it I do, because it is vital to our lives that we have our priorities in order. This means I have to be more conscious of the decisions I am making. When I sit down at the computer, I have to think "Is this really serving a purpose, or am I just procrastinating with regard to something else or someone else?" Do I always get it right? No. I am a work in progress, often having more bad days than good. But I keep trying to get it right. It's been said that at the end of life, no one ever looks back wishing he or she had spent more time at the office. So make time for the relationships and people in your life.

Tony says...

There's no question that we're all busy people. We have family obligations, work, school, projects to do, emails to check, and meetings to attend. And there are only so many hours in the day. So, how are you spending your time? Where are you spending it? Who are you spending it with?

I struggle with these questions, too. There are times I feel overwhelmed by everything I have to do, but then I catch myself watching a football game for two hours. What? I get out of balance and lose focus on what's important. It's something I have to constantly keep in check.

Some years back, I had it all wrong. I had gotten back into road cycling and found myself increasingly obsessed with it. As I began to get more fit, my goals began to get bigger. While I worked to achieve those goals, I pushed aside everything else in my life. My whole life revolved around cycling. Alisa would tell me that I wasn't paying attention to her or the kids, but I didn't hear her – or rather, didn't want to hear her. It was about me and what I wanted to achieve. And it wasn't just my family I neglected. My work and health began to suffer as well. I had over-trained and found myself lethargic, tired, and irritable. Spiritually, I was falling farther away from God. I would miss church on Sunday mornings so I could ride. I was headed for a big fall.

A few months later, that fall came to pass – literally. While I was riding early one morning, a runner stepped out in front of me. I hit her and went flying over my handlebars, ending up with a cracked helmet, scrapes and scratches down my right side, and a busted ego. The crash derailed everything I was striving for, and I was a mess. But I was finally ready to hear what Alisa was trying to tell me. I was missing out on the things that really count. What should have been a hobby had turned into my sole priority.

Are you going through a similar struggle?

If so, don't wait for that proverbial fall to realize that you need to change. It's time to get this thing we call life in order, *from the top down.* If you are neglecting God and your family because of all those other things in your life, here's something you should know: there will always be something else you "have to do." That's not an excuse for not living your life from the top down (God, Spouse, Kids, Work, and other activities, in that order). It's been a couple of years since I learned that lesson, and I can tell you, getting my priorities in order was worth it. My determination to change healed and strengthened my soul, my marriage, and my family. When I do get on the bike, it feels right – because I am finally living life in order, and that is a life that can be used for the Glory of God.

What are you waiting for? Let's get started living *from the top down.*

Journal Entry

Tony: *Don't just pretend to love others. Really love them. Hate what is wrong. Hold tightly to what is good. Love each other with genuine affection, and take delight in honoring each other.*

Romans 12:9-10 (New Living Translation)

The key is not to prioritize what's on your schedule, but to schedule your priorities.

—Stephen R. Covey

Questions

1. List your priorities as you think they are right now.

Work, Family, Other Activities, God, Spouse

Husband   Wife

1._____   1._____

2._____   2._____

3._____   3._____

4._____   4._____

5._____   5._____

2. Grab a calendar and for the next 2 weeks journal 30-minute segments on what you are doing. Fill in each day with the activity you are doing at that time. The five areas you want to fill in are:

- God - Prayer, worship, service

- Spouse - Date nights, talking time, activities together

- Family - Activities as a family

- Work - Full-time, part-time, new business endeavor

- Other Activities - Hobbies, sports, time with friends

3. Where are you spending the majority of your time?
_____ [husband] and_____ [wife]

4. What are three (3) things you can do today that will help you prioritize from the top down?

Husband   Wife

1._____   1._____

2._____   2._____

3._____   3._____

Don't be a time manager, be a priority manager.

—Denis Waitley

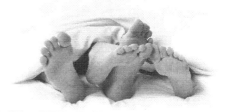

ENOUGH ALREADY! EMOTIONAL INTIMACY

3

We are a society of joiners. From an early age we hear that it's wrong to say no, and yet as we get older it is sometimes the best thing we can do. Have you ever decided against joining a committee? Or maybe you don't want to volunteer for a particular project. What about calling it quits to something you have already said yes to? Is it OK to say no to the outside commitments so that you can say YES to your marriage?

Alisa says...

"Sure, I can help with that!"
"We'd love to come over for dinner."
"It would be great for the kids to do music and sports!"
"No problem, we can fit it in."

Does this sound like your marriage? Too many commitments and not enough time in the day. What if it didn't have to be that way? What if you could make a radical decision to ease the stress?

You can. Just Say **NO**.

Everyone remembers that slogan, and sometimes you have to put it to use in your personal life. It's easy to get wrapped up in all the commitments and obligations that come with work, kids, and other activities. However, when you get so busy that you neglect your marriage, you are neglecting the foundation of your family. It's important to maintain a healthy balance. That means you can't do everything. And if your marriage is strengthened as a result of saying no, isn't that worth it?

When you look at everything on your "To Do" list, do you feel overwhelmed? Is your schedule full of commitments and obligations? Committees? Projects? Volunteering? Friends? I'm not saying any of these things is wrong in and of itself. And I'm not saying that you should drop everything and become a hermit with your spouse.

So… what to do?

Just say NO. It's something that may not come easily at first. After all, we're so accustomed to saying yes. But those three words can truly transform you. "Just Say No" was a great campaign for teaching kids to stay away from drugs, and now, as adults, we can use it to teach ourselves to restore balance to our lives.

Don't get me wrong; it's nice to feel needed. It's flattering to have people depend on us or want to spend time with us. And it is important for our children to become well-rounded citizens. However, each time we add a new activity, meeting, or club, something else is inevitably pushed down on our list of priorities. What's typically the first thing to go? You guessed it: your marriage. You know your spouse will "always be there," so he or she can wait, right? We over-schedule and over-commit, all because we don't know how, or don't want, to say no.

Tony and I have learned to avoid that chaotic lifestyle. How? By simply opting to do two things: 1) We don't say yes to everything we get invited to; and 2) We deprive our kids of an over-scheduled childhood. I can hear the gasps now! But hear me out.

First, we don't attend every birthday party, family function, baby shower, girls' night, etc. Why? Because too much time away begins to erode the foundation of our marriage. Second, we tried lots of different activities with Alex, our firstborn, and it just plain wore me out. Now Alex participates in just two activities, and not on the same night. Abby, our other "deprived" child, has yet to start any type of classes or programs. So what do our kids do? Alex and Abby hang out with us or play with other kids in the neighborhood. We don't participate in every event at school or church, so I don't spend all my time driving around. We make time to just hang out as a foursome.

If you must play, decide on three things at the start: the rules of the game, the stakes and the quitting time.

—Chinese Proverb

Am I telling you that you have to stop doing the things you love or pull your kids out of their favorite activities? Of course not. You wouldn't listen to me even if I did. What I am saying is that you need to evaluate how much energy you are expending on all of this other stuff, and then figure out for yourself whether it's worth it. The answers will be different for everyone.

There will always be something else you "could" do, so you have to draw the line somewhere. The next time someone asks you for help and you hear yourself thinking, "It's just one little thing, I can squeeze it in," remember this: yes, you can squeeze it in – but only if something else gets squeezed out.

Tony says...

I come from a big Italian family. Think *My Big Fat Greek Wedding* - Italian style. But Alisa and I discovered that we had to establish some boundaries. God has blessed us with a wonderful extended family, but we know that our bond as husband and wife is sacred: "For this reason a man will leave his father and mother and be united to his wife, and they will become one flesh." —Genesis 2:24.

Alisa and I married young (ages 22 and 23, respectively), and we didn't understand the necessity of creating a life independent of our parents. What they said or thought was a frequent source of friction. Five years into our marriage, we decided to move from Southern California to the Northwest. It was a marriage-altering experience. Our relationship was now focused on us.

I'm not saying you have to move to another state if you are experiencing similar struggles, but it is imperative to realize that the two of you are the **only** people in your marriage. For us, it took getting away from family to begin to create our own.

 The cold of the Northwest and the desire to raise our children near their grandparents eventually brought us back to Southern California. It wasn't a smooth transition, by any means. I remember the time I had to confront my dad about the boundaries Alisa and I had laid out for our family. He wasn't happy, but he respected our decision. Now my relationship with my dad is the best it has ever been. He is proud of the son, husband, and father I have become. I couldn't have forged that new identity if Alisa and I hadn't vigorously protected our union.

I still draw upon that experience today. Just as we had to remain unwavering with our family boundaries when we returned to Southern California, we have to remain equally resolute about not overloading our family with activities and commitments. We've learned to say no to many great opportunities because we know the burden it would put on our marriage and home life.

You too need to stand up and begin to develop family boundaries. It's time to take back your time so that you can rekindle the intimacy in your marriage.

Journal Entry

Alisa: *Got a birthday invitation today, but we decided to decline so that we could spend time together.*

It's important to set boundaries and ensure that family time takes priority over other things.

—Barbara Schneider

Questions

1. What activities are you involved with each week?

Husband	Wife
1._____	1._____
2._____	2._____
3._____	3._____
4._____	4._____
5._____	5._____

2. If Less is More, what activities are you willing to give up for the next 60 days?

Husband	Wife
1._____	1._____
2._____	2._____
3._____	3._____
4._____	4._____
5._____	5._____

3. Do you function independently of your extended family? If not, what relationships are detrimental to your marriage?

4. What steps do you need to take to create your independent family unit?

You have to set boundaries and say no.

—Jennifer Allyn

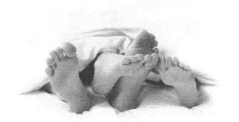

LET'S TALK INTELLECTUAL INTIMACY

4

Prioritizing your time is important to the success of your marriage, as we discovered in the previous section. Communication is crucial, too.

A shrug of the shoulders... a quick passing phrase... maybe even an "uh-uh." Does this pass for communication in your marriage? Do you wish there was something more? Remember when you first met. Hours passed in the blink of an eye as you got to know each other, volleying questions back and forth, filled with an insatiable desire and curiosity to know this person. New relationships are filled with this sharing of thoughts and feelings, history and dreams, and then the relationship begins to settle into routines. Couples take on their "roles," and life becomes more predictable. Unfortunately, communication often becomes predictable, too.

When we stop sharing with our spouse, consciously or unconsciously, we begin to tear down the foundation of our marriage. Communication, true communication, requires sharing our thoughts and feelings with each other. Let's be honest: none of us are mind readers, so ladies, stop expecting your husband to know what you want him to do. Men, invest more time in communicating with your wife. Most women love to talk, and taking the time to communicate with her will dramatically change the tone of your marriage for the better.

Alisa says...

When was the last time you had a meaningful conversation with your spouse? Sure, you may talk a lot, but do you ever get past a rundown of the day?

"Honey, can you pick up milk on the way home?"

"Alex has a program at school tonight; don't be late."

"Abby was acting up today."

Take a minute and think about this. Do you know your spouse's fears? Do you know what he/she dreams about? How long has it been since you sat down without any distractions and had a deep conversation?

The answer is probably that it's been too long. Tony and I have cycled through periods in our marriage when communication was sorely lacking, practically nonexistent. If I didn't want to discuss something, I would just shut down and gave my pat response: "I'm fine" (translation: leave me alone). Great way to talk to your husband, isn't it?

It's not always easy living with another person, but nurturing your lines of communication is critical. Whether you're blowing off your spouse or falling into the trap of discussing only surface issues, breakdowns in communication are destructive. One or both spouses may feel:

- Isolated
- Distant
- Lonely
- Frustrated
- Angry
- Sad

That's the bad news. Now for the good news: you *can* stop this cycle and change your relationship for the better. It won't be easy, but then again, no one ever said marriage was. (If they did, they were lying to you.)

So let's get started.

Commit to each other (not just to yourself – you have to verbalize it) that you are going to make meaningful communication the priority in your marriage. Why does it

Communication is depositing a part of yourself in another person.

—Anonymous

have to be the priority? Because if you are not communicating, you are not growing. You are not being intimate. And without that, you are only scratching the surface of what your marriage can be.

I'm a wife, a mother, a daughter, and a sister, so I know what it's like to feel like you have no time to spare. Still, you have to make time every day to sit with your spouse and really talk. You can keep it short and simple, just discussing a couple of the most important things that happened that day and what is on your mind. If you are listening, don't talk; focus on what your spouse is saying (and isn't saying). If you are the sharing spouse, get past the "surface stuff" and share from your heart. If it seems like you haven't had this kind of conversations since your dating days, it may feel awkward and uncomfortable at first. It takes practice, but it is so worth it!

I know that because Tony and I have worked hard to get to this point. Now, when he asks me what's going on, I tell him the whole truth, even if I don't want to, because I know it's the right thing for our marriage. By telling him, I allow Tony to get closer to me and our relationship to deepen.

Now it's your turn to become ONE.

Tony says...

Alisa and I met while she was participating in an internship program at the University of Colorado at Boulder. I had been hired by the internship program to be a cook at the fraternity house where she was living for the summer. The World Cup was on TV, and we found ourselves watching it together and talking quite a bit. And we really didn't stop talking in the weeks and months that followed. I wanted to know everything about her. Where did she grow up? What was her family like? What was she studying? We chatted as we walked in the park or along Boulder Creek that summer. We were infatuated with each other, holding hands, hugging, and kissing as we found out more and more about each other. We couldn't get enough.

As the years passed, the business of everyday life began to take precedence over the soul-searching talks. We grew apart, and tension wore us down. When we did talk, the conversations usually got heated, and in the process Alisa would shut down. I would try to engage her with questions and conversation, but the most I would get was a head nod.

How had we gone from an insatiable yearning to hear every word the other had to say to not being able to speak to each other without fighting? There was no more talk of our dreams, passions, and desires. Our conversations revolved around bills, work, and the mundane. We no longer delved into each other's souls, as if fearful that what we might find something about each other that would drive us further apart.

Climbing out of that kind of low point is similar to climbing a mountain. There are many switchbacks and stumbling blocks along the way, but you know the views from the top are worth it. Is your marriage worth it? Do you want to see the glory from the top of the mountain? If so, you are in the right place. If you've made it this far, you've taken the first step to regaining the loving communication you desire.

Alisa suggested taking the time to talk with your spouse, without distractions, each day. Do it. It will make the hike to that mountaintop so much easier. Turn off the TV, get the kids to bed, hold hands, and tell your spouse the three most important dreams, desires, or fears you have today. Do it! Don't wait another night. Feels uncomfortable, you say? Sure it does. Revealing our innermost selves makes us vulnerable, and not many people like that feeling.

To this day, when I have something big to discuss with Alisa, my hands get sweaty and my heart thumps in my chest. Yet each time, I find that it was worth pushing through my fears. She gets to know all of me, as a wife should. The best part is that our physical intimacy has become more fulfilling. Our overall intimacy has soared. Committing to deep conversation has made our bedroom a place where we give wings to our passions and desires.

It's time to make your move. Don't sit on the sidelines any longer. The entire marital experience is based on communication. So dig deep, ask questions, and watch as your bond grows stronger than ever before.

During this time of openness and discovery, you need to answer each question truthfully, honestly, and from the heart. This is a time to go deep in your marriage as you connect with one another.

The single biggest problem in communication is the illusion that it has taken place.

—George Bernard Shaw

Journal Entries

Alisa: *The kids have been at mom and dad's all weekend, which has given us a little more flexibility and a lot more in the way of conversation. We have been able to really sit down and dig deep these last couple of days.*

Tony: *We began this evening again with Alisa talking and me listening. This is Alisa's time to open up and my time to listen to her. Listening to her has really made a difference in just three days. Who would have thought by just listening there would arise such passion between us? We talked for a long time this evening, so by the time we got to making love it was a quickie.*

Questions

1. What three (3) questions can you ask each other to foster openness and discovery over the next 60 days?

Husband

1._____

2._____

3._____

Wife

1._____

2._____

3._____

2. What qualities in our marriage allow us to have good communication?

3. What distractions have diverted you from interacting with each other?

4. What do we do in our marriage to have great communication? Be specific.

Some conversations are uncomfortable but necessary for a healthy marriage.

—Richard Nicastro, Ph.D.

www.StrengthenYourRelationship.com

MONEY MATTERS
FINANCIAL
INTIMACY

5

We've been discussing the importance of communication. One way to unlock intimacy in your marriage is for you and your spouse to talk about your finances, your money. You can't hide behind credit card juggling and hidden purchases. The two of you must decide how much money is needed each month for the family to live. Doing this together is a great way to settle differences, if there are any, and can improve your relationship. Financial stress is an intimacy killer, and one of the leading causes of divorce.

As ONE, you must distribute financial responsibilities to each other. Your decisions should be based more on one another's capabilities, means and interests than on outdated stereotypes based on gender. Years ago, a man was to "bring home the bacon" and the woman was to stay in the house to take care of the children. Depending on your family, this scenario may or may not work today.

In our marriage, we both worked in the early years when we didn't have kids. After having our first child, Alisa stayed home while I worked. With this life change we had to change our financial plan as well. No longer could we be completely carefree with our money. I was now responsible for making sure our financial needs were met through my work. At the end of each month Alisa and I would sit down and prepare a budget. It took us a few months of trial and to come up with a plan we could live with. Once we had that plan, implementation became routine. We began to discuss our finances on a regular basis. Each month we gave ourselves "Blow" Money. This is money that we could spend anywhere we wanted, any way we wanted, without having to tell each other. Large financial decisions are made jointly. Are we perfect at this? NO! But each month we make our budget a priority so that our money doesn't get in the way of our intimacy.

In the days before we devised our financial plan, Alisa and I never knew how much or who was spending what. It caused a lot of anxiety, which led to the bedroom.

Once we were on the same page with our finances, the difference in how we reacted to each other changed dramatically.

Every family's needs and abilities will be different, and you need to decide on the best scenario for yours. Share any events, especially financial ones, with each other, and make sure that important decisions are discussed and mutually agreed upon with one another's best interest in mind.

With money, there are two options: A) Spend first and then make a plan, or B) Plan first and then spend. It is entirely your choice, but having done both we can say, without a doubt, that planning first makes for a much happier marriage. It will feel awkward at first, but planning ahead enables the two of you to know what you need, beyond just what you want. Planning also enhances your creativity, as it forces you to think of innovative and often better ways to cover expenses. Make those financial changes in your marriage and watch your intimacy soar.

Alisa says...

What couple hasn't argued over money? Financial issues are at the root of many marital conflicts, and can sap intimacy in a hurry. So make time to get on the same financial page as your spouse. No secrets allowed.

Money matters can be very hard for couples to discuss. People learn financial habits from their parents, and frequently bring two very different approaches into their marriage. Money can be such a volatile topic that a lot of couples don't even discuss finances – or if they do, it often ends up in a shouting match. When I was growing up,

You must tell your spouse everything about your debt, income, financial strengths and weaknesses. No secrets allowed.

—Dave Ramsey

my parents never really talked about money. It seemed like the ATM had an endless supply of $20 bills. I can still see my dad sitting down at the table a couple of times a month to pay the bills. Even though I was encouraged to work, and did, starting with babysitting at age 11, I never really learned how to manage my money. For me, money just allowed me to buy the things I wanted when I wanted them, instead of having to ask my parents. For my family, our finances became a major issue when my parents filed bankruptcy while I was in high school and we subsequently lost our house. I remember creditors calling, and telling them that my parents weren't home, because they didn't want to take the calls. I can still see the basket on our front step the one year that we received a turkey dinner for Thanksgiving. It definitely colored my perception of finances and how I wanted my married life to be, even though early on Tony and I still didn't know how to take control of our money.

Think about this. Have you ever purchased something knowing you were going to keep the purchase from your spouse? Do you sometimes break up the cost of your purchases between different credit cards so your husband or wife won't notice the total damage? Do you find yourself making irresponsible spending decisions? Has keeping up with your friends and neighbors gotten you into a world of financial trouble? Years ago, my answers to these questions were all YES!

Money issues are detrimental to intimacy. When times are tough financially in your marriage, with creditors calling and bills left unpaid, worry and fear can overtake your affection for one another. Keeping secrets about money has the same effect. Hiding purchases or spending money you don't have erodes the foundation of your relationship.

How do we know? Well, the early years of our marriage were riddled with monetary mistakes. As financial guru Dave Ramsey says on his popular radio show, "We did stupid, with lots of zeros."

Tony and I essentially lived off our credit cards, figuring we were doing OK as long as we could make the minimum payments each month. We financed almost the entire cost of our cars, and spent every penny we made keeping up with friends – on the heels of a year's worth of travel while we were in a long-distance relationship. After a few years of marriage, we found ourselves some $50,000 in debt. I dreaded getting the mail, knowing it would bring only more bills. For a long time, we didn't talk about money, but eventually, the situation got so bad we were forced into credit counseling. At that point, there was no way to avoid the subject.

In the fall of 2001, we left Southern California for Spokane, Washington, and a simpler way of life. Tony and I cut back and focused on getting debt-free. Even during the worst Spokane winters, we piled on the blankets instead of bumping up the thermostat. That meant six to eight blankets! We had no TV, no cable. We didn't go out to eat much. I shopped at thrift stores and clearance racks (still do – I love a bargain). Every month my paycheck went to pay down our debt while we lived off Tony's income. I cannot tell you how liberating it was to make the final payments. We were finally free of debt, and free to rebuild the areas of our marriage torn down by the financial stress.

We have since moved back to Southern California, and now the only outstanding debt we have is our mortgage. We know where our money is going each month, and we are able to tithe, save, and have discretionary income. We do not make financial decisions without talking to each other. Big purchases require saving; we do not use credit cards because of the potential for overspending. Money is something we now discuss openly, and we came to realize we should have been discussing it all along. By not facing our financial issues head-on, we perpetuated the problem and allowed it to drive a wedge between us. Today, the absence of financial secrets or tensions enables us to experience deeper intimacy in our marriage.

Tony says...

If you and your spouse aren't on the same page financially, prepare for a rocky road. It's one of the most contentious scenarios: one person spends and the other saves. One is working on a cash flow plan; the other is blowing the plan to pieces. It's a stress that pervades almost every aspect of life.

When Alisa and I were first married, we were on the same page – just not a good one. We did a poor job of managing our money. As Alisa mentioned, years of overspending, student loans, car loans, and a near total dependence on credit cards left us in serious debt. We made so many stupid mistakes about our finances that it was uncomfortable to discuss the situation. So we didn't.

Ignoring a problem doesn't make it go away, but following some sage advice can. Driving around Spokane one fall afternoon, I came across the Dave Ramsey Show on the radio. From the moment I heard Dave speak, I knew his advice could make a difference in our marriage. It was like Dave was giving us the roadmap to becoming

Owe nothing to anyone – except for your obligation to love one another.

—Romans 13:8

debt-free. I listened for weeks, learning how Dave's Baby Steps were helping normal people like Alisa and I get out of debt. The more I heard, the more I began to build up the courage to talk with Alisa. Using Dave's advice as a guide, I formulated a plan to get us out of debt, and the next day, I shared my thoughts with Alisa. She was taken aback; after all, from her viewpoint my plan had come out of nowhere.

She began to listen to the Dave Ramsey show, too, and we read Dave's book, *Financial Peace*. It wasn't an easy road; in fact, it was a tough time for us. We had to sacrifice to get to the light at the end of our tunnel. As Alisa mentioned, we went without heat in our apartment, to the point where we could see our breath inside. But every sacrifice took us closer to living debt-free, and we eventually got there.

While no one wants to endure financial struggles, that time was a turning point in our marriage. We learned to work together in a potentially divisive area and built the financial intimacy we have today. Financial intimacy lays the groundwork for a more fulfilling marriage.

Questions

1. When was the last time you looked at your finances together?

2. Do your money issues rob you of intimacy? Why?

3. How much debt do you have, excluding mortgage?

4. What plan of action must you take to rid yourselves of consumer debt?

Stop spending

Cut up the credit cards

Live on cash

Build an Emergency Fund

5. Does giving to our church, a non-profit organization, or someone in need involve a risk-taking mentality on our part?

Those who love money will never have enough. How absurd to think that wealth brings true happiness!

—Ecclesiastes 5:10

WHAT DO WE DO NOW? RECREATIONAL INTIMACY

6

As married couples, there are times when we get caught up in unconscious routines. Think about your week: from morning to night, Monday until Sunday, everything seems to repeat itself. You go to work in the morning; you come home from work in the afternoon; you watch TV, play video games or sit at the computer; and then, you go to bed to do it all over again. Sound familiar? We feel penned in, and we tend to get frustrated, annoyed, and angry with our spouse because we have stopped connecting or growing. This is the time when the two of you should realize that you need to explore other areas of interest to get out of your rut. It's a time to laugh, dance, break free from the day-to-day and reenergize your marriage.

Alisa says...

Take the time to figure out what you like to do together, and then do it!

Tony is an avid road cyclist, and I love to read. He's more of a people person, whereas I like my quiet time. I like to shop and he doesn't. Get the picture? No matter how close you are as a couple, we all have our own hobbies and activities that don't overlap with those of our spouse.

Whether you are newly married or have been at this for quite some time, you must figure out how you can spend time together doing things you both enjoy. The quality of your marriage depends on it.

Enter the **Top 10 List**. This idea was first suggested to us by the family pastors at our church. Here's how it works: You each jot down a list of 10 things you like to do or would like to try. Don't work together on this part. Once you finish, sit down together and share your lists to see what overlaps. Don't have anything in common? Try it again. Come up with another five or ten ideas. Keep going until you come up with a couple of activities you would both enjoy. If you haven't come up with any matches, keep at it until you do. And yes, for those who are asking, sex does count!

Here is the challenging part for busy couples: You have to make time to *do* those things. It's not enough to know that you would both like to go to a musical. Find out when one is playing, get a sitter, and go on a date! If hiking is on the list, lace up your shoes and pull out the sunscreen and water bottles. The purpose is to deepen your relationship by spending time together and exploring new and different activities. If there is something on your spouse's list that you've never considered but that sounds like it might be worth trying, take the plunge.

When we first started dating, Tony suggested that we go hiking. Now, I am a city girl from Ohio. No mountains. But I really wanted to spend time with Tony and get to know him better, so of course I agreed. Hiking in the Colorado Mountains is tough, but we did have some of the most amazing conversations in those mountains, and it turned out that I really liked hiking – to an extent. You too may have to be open to trying something new in order to get back in "couple mode." Just remember to be considerate of your spouse when he or she is trying something you like to do.

Comparing your lists may help you get to know your husband or wife better, too. The first time Tony and I did this exercise, we found out that we both like plays and musicals. We were going on a decade of marriage at that point, and had no idea we had that in common. It just goes to show that you continue to learn and grow throughout your marriage. All it takes is a willingness to make time for each other.

Life lived amidst tension and busyness needs leisure. Leisure that recreates and renews. Leisure should be a time to think new thoughts...

—C. Neil Straight

Tony says...

The Top 10 List is by far one of my favorite things to do with Alisa. In a marriage, you can get so wrapped up in the things you have to do that you neglect the things you want to do. Taking the opportunity to do some of the things on your "wish list" brings you closer together and relieves stress. This time together pays dividends for your relationship – if you approach it the right way.

I approached it the wrong way in the early years of our marriage. I am all about the outdoors, so I was thrilled when Alisa agreed to hike and backpack the Southern California trails and the Sierra Nevada Mountain Range. We had a great time preparing for our hikes, working together to plan our meals and gather our gear. But once we got out on the trail, I was 20 steps ahead of her and pushing her to go faster.

Once, we went to Yosemite National Park for four days. It was absolutely beautiful – lush meadows and secluded camping. Unfortunately, Alisa got altitude sickness. I was enjoying myself so much that I forgot this was "together" time. She wanted to go home; I was determined to push forward, not really caring how Alisa felt. This was my vacation, for heaven's sake. So we hiked on. I had the recreation down, just not the intimacy. I learned a tough lesson on that trip. My desire to accomplish my goals was more important than my relationship with my wife. It didn't hit me until much later, but once it did I viewed our time together differently.

By the grace of God, Alisa didn't give up on hiking and backpacking after that trip. We sat down and talked about how to make the experience more pleasurable for both of us. We decided that I would hike behind Alisa, and instead of pushing her to go faster, I would encourage her. A year after our trip to Yosemite, we did a 3-day, 40-mile backpacking trip in Sequoia and Kings Canyon National Park. The high point was when we topped out at 11,978 feet at Glen Pass. It was a high point for our relationship as well, as we began to understand the wonderful impact recreational intimacy can exert on a marriage.

This doesn't mean you have to do everything together. As Alisa mentioned, I love road cycling and she doesn't. Alisa likes digital scrap booking and I don't. But we still pull out our Top 10 List and make a point to find new things we want to do as a couple. Even if there are plenty of things you do together – errands, kids' soccer games, whatever – you need to also find activities that allow you to focus on your relationship. They can be simple things: we make time for long walks, road trips, and college football on a Saturday afternoon. These are chances to relax and enjoy each other's company, and to reflect back as well as look forward. We put everything aside for one another.

Try it. After all, doesn't your spouse deserve some quality time?

Outdoor/Physical Activities

Going for a Walk

Jogging

Backpacking/Car Camping

Hiking

Picnicking

Canoeing

Racquetball

Volleyball

Rollerblading/Ice Skating

Explore the Local/National/State Park

Swimming in the pool

Going to the Beach/Lake

Frisbee

Pass the Football (Nerf)

Basketball

Bike Rides

Skiing/Snowboarding

Bowling

Golfing/Driving Range

Miniature Golfing

Flying a Kite

Inviting Friends to play Laser Tag or Paintball

Ballroom Dancing

Getting Out of the House

Live College Sports Events

The Symphony, Plays, Ballet, or Opera

Rock Concerts

Going Out for Dinner

Going Out to See a Movie

Going Out for Ice Cream

Going for a Scenic Drive

Having Lunch Together on a Work Day

Window Shopping

Going to the Mall

Yard Sale/Garage Sale/Antiquing

Amusement Park

Aquarium/Museum/Cultural Tour

Going for a Walk along the Beach, Lake, or River

Staying In

Cooking Dinner Together

Inviting Friends Over for Dinner

Baking Cookies/Desserts Together

Renting a Movie

Scrabble

Yahtzee

Cribbage

Trivial Pursuit

Backgammon

Reading on the Couch Together

Sketching Each Other's Portrait

Playing with Pets/Taking Them for a Walk

Need for Relaxation

Taking a Nap

Day Spa

Hot bath/Jacuzzi

Backrubs

Romantic

Candlelight Dinner

Stargazing

Watching the Sunset/Sunrise

Taking a Trip

Weekend Bed and Breakfast

Fun/Exotic Vacation Travel

Road Trip

Visiting Close Friends or Family

This list is not exhaustive, but a starter to get your mind moving in the right direction.

Journal Entries

Alisa: *I relish our time together doing an activity we both enjoy. I am reminded of the love and comfort I find only from him.*

Tony: *We went to dinner with some good friends. Great conversation during dinner, and afterwards we walked on the beach in La Jolla. A perfect setting to get in the mood. Best part was that the kids were at the grandparents' for the weekend. We were able to enjoy the lovemaking process with no concerns of kids interrupting us.*

We enjoy cooking and share cooking responsibilities. We cook as much for recreation as to eat.

—Rick Boucher

Questions

1. Top 10 List Worksheet –
http://www.oneextraordinarymarriage
.com/stripped-down-resources

2. What are the Top 3 activities you would like to do together?

1.

2.

3.

3. Where in your schedules can you carve out time to be active together?

4. What activities take your mind off your troubles?

If bread is the first necessity of life, recreation is a close second.

—Edward Bellamy

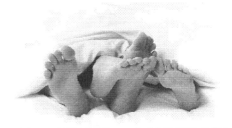

CALENDAR "IT" EMOTIONAL INTIMACY

7

What's on your calendar?

- Daily in-depth conversation with your spouse
- Daily devotionals together
- Recreational activities you both enjoy
- Date Night
- Making love

Scheduling time with your spouse is just as important as scheduling the rest of your obligations, if not more so. You've already established your priorities; now it's time to put that into action. After years of marriage, it's easy to allow your life to become routine. Sure, you enjoy spending time with your spouse, but are you actively keeping your connection alive?

Alisa says...

You schedule your work appointments and doctor visits, but do you deliberately set aside time for your spouse? Make intimacy a priority and put it on the calendar.

Here's my typical weekly calendar: taking the kids to Tae Kwon Do class (twice), hosting a small group at our church, my moms' group, doctor appointments, play dates, volunteer work… and the list goes on. Sound familiar?

If your calendar looks anything like mine, you probably have just about every hour of the day planned to include your job, your children's school and extra-curricular activities, keeping up with your husband's schedule, and all of the other stuff that comes with living in such a fast-paced, plugged-in world. We've already talked about how our calendars reflect our priorities. So shouldn't your spouse be on there? I know, it sounds a little silly. You may be thinking, *I live with my spouse. Why do I need to put him on my calendar? I tell him I love him, and I do things for him. Doesn't he know he's important?*

Here's what you need to remember: It's not just about spending time with your spouse; it's about spending *quality* time with your spouse. When Tony and I started focusing on getting quality time together, our marriage took a 180-degree turn. Before, spending time with Tony generally happened at the end of the day, when the kids were in bed and we had nothing else to do. By that point, I was so tired that I wasn't truly engaged with him. Sex wasn't that important. If I wasn't in the mood, then too bad. Looking back, I see that although I was married to Tony, I wasn't committed to really being ONE with my husband.

Marriage requires effort. It requires making a commitment, and not just on the day you become husband and wife. It's about a commitment to continually grow, to learning about and with your spouse. And you can't do that if you're not making time for each other.

So now, my husband is on my calendar. We have date nights, and we also schedule some "together time" during daylight hours. (If you only have time for each other at night, you know one or both of you will fall asleep!) We take advantage of the times when the kids are out playing with their friends to sit and talk.

And yes, we do schedule physical intimacy (sex) – not the specific day and time, but rather, windows of opportunity. We split the week in half, each taking three days (Saturday is rest day). We each agree to initiate sex on one of our days. This "schedule" has made intimacy a priority again in our relationship. It ensures that we are regularly making love, which is a kind of glue that bonds us.

The hours I spend with you I look upon as sort of a perfumed garden, a dim twilight, and a fountain singing to it. You and you alone make me feel that I am alive. Other men it is said have seen angels, but I have seen thee and thou art enough.

—George Moore

This agreement also took the responsibility for initiating physical intimacy off of Tony's shoulders. I had fallen into the habit of making him ask for it, then playing my power card – Do I or don't I feel like having sex? It was all about what I wanted, and that wasn't fair. It took me a long time to realize that those times I repeatedly said NO made him feel rejected and severely bruised our relationship.

Following our new intimacy lifestyle removed a source of potential stress in our marriage. Tony knows that if he makes an advance on one of his three days, I am going to say YES, even if it is in part because I know he won't be after me on the other nights (yes, I still get tired). But it demonstrates to my husband that he is a priority, and that no matter what is going on, I am committed to making love to him regularly.

Having physical intimacy twice a week may be a huge leap for you right now. What if you alternated weeks instead of days? Whatever time frame you work with, what would happen if physical intimacy became more of a constant in your relationship? How would things be different if your spouse saw his name on your calendar?

Tony says...

I'd never considered putting "IT" on the calendar before Alisa and I had kids. In those days, we had a date night every week. We'd stay out all night and sleep late on Saturday morning – no one to think about but us. Of course, that changes when you have kids. When our children were little, Alisa and I had trouble finding the right balance. I remember struggling with a lot of anger issues because I wasn't able to get away with Alisa like I had in the past. I missed being with just her. One evening, Alisa and I talked, and I discovered that she missed me, too. So we made a commitment to dating again. Our sitter offers "First Friday Night," inviting a number of kids over to her house for pizza and a movie every month, freeing up moms and dads to go on dates. At least once a month, we have that time to totally focus on each other.

Over the years, our calendars have become full with family events, work, church functions, sports, and a host of other "To Do" items. I know what it means to feel like you have no time to spare: I have two kids, lead a small group at our church, am self-employed, volunteer, and am very active outdoors. Believe me, I know the strains and stresses you are under. But wouldn't it be worth it to schedule some "alone time" with your spouse?

Calendar "IT" was our way of bringing an end to those days of non-stop activities, of putting everything else first. When we committed to making love for two months straight, we realized we had to make time for each other and for physical intimacy, or it wasn't going to happen. There's nothing wrong with scheduling time for your spouse, just like you do with all those other important things in your life. Do a date night once a month, choose a morning to kick back at the coffee shop, or maybe stroll through the park. Whatever you do, just do it! Get it on the calendar, get the babysitter, and get together.

Journal Entries

Alisa: *Abby's doing better. Tony called our sitter to see if the kids can still do 1st Friday Night. She said yes. Yeah!!! We went to our favorite sushi place in town and came home afterward and watched a movie.*

Tony: *First Friday Night. It wasn't going to happen this month with Alex and Abby sick, but I felt good and Abby was doing better. Our babysitter was OK taking the kids, so Alisa and I took her up on it. Glad we did. Alisa and I went out to our favorite sushi spot to celebrate our 12th Wedding Anniversary. We prayed tonight to our amazing God.*

Love one another and you will be happy. It's as simple and as difficult as that.

—Michael Leunig

Questions

1. What do we need to change in our schedules to make more time for us?

2. What would you like to do on our next date night?

3. How do you feel about us scheduling sex? What would you look forward to? What would concern you?

4. Who most often initiates sex in our relationship? How does that make you feel?

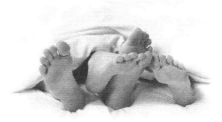

TAKE THE LEAD
INTELLECTUAL
INTIMACY

8

There are so many decisions we have to make on a daily basis, not just for ourselves but for those for whom we are responsible. Sometimes we just get tired, or maybe even lazy, and stop making decisions where they really make a difference – in our marriage. Have you stopped making the decisions in your relationship? Have you become apathetic toward your spouse, both in and out of the bedroom? It's time to shake things up and Take the Lead.

Alisa says...

After 11 years of marriage, this is what date night sounded like:

"What do you want to do?"

"I don't know. What do you want to do?"

"I don't know, how about…"

"No, how about..."

"Fine, that works."

Were our regular date nights filled with excitement and anticipation? No. Instead, they had a level of resignation to them. Not exactly the formula for romance, except that the kids were at the sitter's.

If you've been married any length of time, this probably sounds familiar. Remember when you were dating, and your spouse would come and pick you up with the night planned? You knew what time your evening would begin, where you were going to eat, and what you were going to do after dinner. What happened to that?

Sometimes it feels like I spend all day making decisions for myself and the kids, and then Tony wants to know what I want to do on date night. My answer? Surprise me!

It wasn't just date night that was getting the short end of the stick. Our sex life suffered, too. I became comfortable letting Tony initiate sex, to the point that he could probably count on one hand the number of times in a year that I made the first move.

We had a number of conversations about changing that – conversations that went something like this: "Alisa, it would be great if you would just initiate sex once in a while." I'd respond, "Uh-huh." Then nothing would change. Finally, we realized we were going to have to do more than just talk about it. Real change would require real effort. So we started an exercise we call "Taking the Lead." This means each of us has designated nights to plan a date or initiate sex. On my nights, I am totally in charge. I decide where we are going for dinner and what else might be on the agenda. If it's my night to initiate sex, I wear my sexy pajamas and light candles. On these nights, Tony doesn't have to do anything except enjoy the experience. And then he takes charge on his nights.

Take our thirteenth anniversary, for example. Tony took the kids to the sitter for the night, as planned, and as he was leaving, he told me there was an envelope for me on the bed. Inside was a romantic card along with our schedule for the evening. He had arranged a massage for me at the house, followed by dinner and a walk along the beach. After my luxurious massage, Tony selected the clothes he wanted me to wear and we headed to our favorite sushi restaurant, where I discovered he had called ahead and pre-ordered dinner. I could not wipe the smile off of my face! Why? Because I did not have to decide anything more complicated than whether I should drink iced tea or water. It was all about making me feel special.

Do not go where the path may lead, go instead where there is no path and leave a trail.

—Ralph Waldo Emerson

Not every date needs to be this elaborate – a little effort goes a long way. These days, we all have so many responsibilities that it's nice to have our spouse to take care of us from time to time, asking nothing in return.

When we first start dating, we woo our partners, court them, and do things with and for them. Don't let the craziness of life allow that to fade away.

Tony says...

In the early days of our dating life, I made it a point to take the lead with Alisa. I decided where we would eat, I'd buy flowers, and I would even let her know the attire for the night. I can still remember our first date, dinner at a nice Chinese restaurant with a great patio overlooking Boulder Creek. I made the decisions because I wanted to take care of her. That first summer was much like our first date.

As the months turned into years, I quit taking the lead. It turned into that classic back-and-forth: "What do you want to do?" By the time we finally went somewhere, we were irritated to the point of ruining the mood. Something had to change if we wanted to experience a deeper level of intimacy. One evening, Alisa and I began to discuss this frustration and came up with "Take the Lead," each committing to taking the initiative on our designated date nights.

As Alisa mentioned, our 13th anniversary happened to be my night. I set up the babysitter ahead of time, made reservations at the restaurant and pre-ordered all of our food, arranged a massage for Alisa, bought a card, drew up our schedule (see below), and reserved a nice car for the weekend. This took time, thought, and effort. It wasn't easy to get it all together, but I love my wife. She is worth it.

Our 13th Wedding Anniversary

Friday, October 3rd, 2009

5:00pm – Kids to Deanna

5:30pm – 1-hour massage for Alisa

7:15pm – Dinner and Dessert

9:00pm – Walk along the beach

Saturday, October 4th, 2009

Sleep in

Breakfast for two

Watch college football

"Take the Lead" will change the dynamic of your marriage by making physical intimacy and dates special again. No more back-and-forth about where to go or what to do, no waiting for your spouse to initiate intimacy. Taking the Lead has eliminated frustration from our date nights, our physical intimacy, and our lives, allowing us to truly enjoy the time we spend together.

Journal Entries

Alisa: *Our first night, and I took the initiative to lay out a blanket and candles on our living room floor. Tony was so surprised!*

Tony: *Alisa and I relaxed all morning long. With the kids away, it was a perfect time to take it easy and enjoy some college football. Alisa and I are big fans of NCAA football, but rarely get the opportunity to watch a game together. Watching football led to caresses and touches, and that progressed to another fantastic lovemaking session in our living room. Can't remember the last time we utilized our living room like this.*

...just take charge and create the experience you are looking for.

—Eric Allenbaugh

Questions

1. Am I willing to let go and let you Take the Lead? Why or why not?

2. What most excites you about having me Take the Lead?

3. Who's Taking the Lead on our next Date Night?

I actually was able to go out there like I own it. To take charge feels good.

—Emanuel Sandhu

GET PHYSICAL
RECREATIONAL
INTIMACY

9

We turn now to another aspect of sharing life as a married couple: getting physical!

Getting physical doesn't just refer to the activities you do together, though engaging in activities with one another is a great way to share, and has the added benefit of increasing your physical health and overall outlook. Getting physical can also encompass activities you engage in to make yourself look and feel better for your spouse.

Everyone knows exercise is good for you. The reality is that we often feel too busy to squeeze in one more thing. So… what to do? Find those activities that you enjoy and allow you to engage in physical activity, whether alone or together. Make a commitment to get into the best possible shape for you and your spouse. Do you have time to sit and watch TV? Then you have time to get physical.

If you don't have the habit of being physically active, this change in your lifestyle will have a dramatic effect not just on your perception of yourself – the whole "look better, feel better" mentality – but also on your spouse's perception of you. Actively investing in improving your physical self is investing in your marriage as well. Wouldn't you like to be your spouse's ideal of beauty? You can, if you will take the initiative to invest in your health and well being.

Alisa says...

Take the time to get your body into the best shape possible. You will appreciate how you look and feel, and your personal satisfaction is likely to spill over to create an amazing response from your spouse.

Aside from a couple of seasons of T-ball as a child, I'd never considered myself an athlete. (Is T-ball athletic? Hmm....) My physical activity has generally consisted of walking and hiking. Tony, on the other hand, is an avid cyclist. We're not talking about casual rides around the block. In each of the last three years, he has completed the California Triple Crown, which means he's done three 200-mile bike rides within the calendar year. And in case you are wondering, he does the entire 200 miles in a single day.

When Tony and I met in college, we were both sporting the freshman 15, plus the sophomore 15, and maybe a few extra pounds thrown in for good measure. After we left college (and the requisite late-night eating and drinking), we started to slim down. Our weight loss accelerated when we started hiking together. We crested the three highest peaks in Southern California and took extended backpacking trips. And then Tony got back into cycling, mountain climbing, and other strenuous physical activities while I was pregnant and working at a desk job.

As I said, I had never made physical activity a priority, and that didn't change much after having kids. After the kids were born I slimmed down fairly easily, but I didn't have the stamina or the energy I wanted. When Alex started taking *Tae Kwon Do* in 2008, I was intrigued. About five months after he started, the instructor began offering a moms' class, and while I was a bit reluctant, I decided I would at least try it. I'm hooked! I like the physicality and the mental challenges, but I love what *Tae Kwon Do* has done for my sex life. Yes, I did say that exercise has improved my sex life! Since starting *Tae Kwon Do*, I'm more muscular and toned. *I* find my body more attractive, and Tony does, too.

Exercise is an individual thing. The mere fact that all of your friends run doesn't mean you are going to like running. Don't join a gym if you would rather ride a bike or hike trails. If you don't know what form of exercise would fit you best, take a class or two in something you have never tried. It just might turn out to be exactly what you are looking for.

Movement is a medicine for creating change in a person's physical, emotional, and mental states.

—www.acefitness.org

You've heard that your body is a temple. Keep that in mind. How you treat your body will affect not only how *you* think about it, but how your spouse responds to you as well. Find an exercise or activity that works for you, and get moving. Trust me, your spouse will notice, and you will both reap the benefits.

Tony says...

It was another routine evening, sitting at home watching TV and doing nothing. Burned out from commuting to work, working all day, and commuting home, Alisa and I didn't have the energy to do anything beyond sitting on the couch. The college years and the early years of our marriage hadn't been beneficial to my waistline, and it was time for something to change.

That night, we made a pact to lose weight. We turned off the television, put on our tennis shoes, and stepped out to walk around our neighborhood. We didn't get far that first night; after a twenty-minute walk, we were spent. But it was a start. The miles began to add up and the pounds began to drop as we explored new areas around our apartment complex. And it helped more than our weight; our walks gave us a much needed opportunity to really talk. There weren't any distractions as we discussed the things that were going on in our lives. In the years since those evening walks we've found other activities we enjoy, together and on our own, but we still find time every now and then to just go for a walk.

I find it amazing when people tell me they don't have the time to exercise. Making the time to work out will benefit you in ways you've probably never imagined.

After studying more than 31,000 men, Harvard School of Public Health researchers reported that those who were physically active had a 30% lower risk of erectile dysfunction than the men who engaged in little or no physical activity.

Women reap the benefits of exercise, too. One study by the University of British Columbia found that 20 minutes of exercise spurred greater sexual response in the women participants as compared with those who engaged in no exercise at all.

It's time to stop wishing and start doing. Do you want to make a positive difference in your marriage and your health? Start doing something that stimulates you physically today. Go. Do. Be active.

Wondering what you can try? Here's a list of ideas to get you started. Remember, keeping your body in good physical shape impacts not only you, but those around you as well.

Aerobics
Archery
Badminton
Baseball
Basketball
Baton Twirling
Bicycling
Billiards
Bowling
Boxing/Kickboxing
Calisthenics
Canoeing
Cardio Machines
Cheerleading
Children's Games
Circuit Training
Cricket
Croquet
Cross Country Skiing
Curling
Dancing
Darts
Diving
Downhill Skiing
Fencing
Fishing
Football
Frisbee
Gardening
Golf
Gymnastics
Hacky Sack
Handball
Hang Gliding

Hiking/Backpacking
Hockey
Home Repair
Horseback Riding
Horseshoe Pitching
Household Tasks
Hunting
Inline Skating
Jai Alai
Juggling
Kayaking
Lacrosse
Lawn Bowling
Lifting/Hauling
Marching
Martial Arts
Motor Cross
Mountain Biking
Mountain Climbing
Orienteering
Paddleball
Pedometer
Pilates
Polo
Racquetball
Rock Climbing
Roller Skating
Rope Jumping
Rowing
Rugby
Running
Sailing
Scuba Diving
Shuffleboard

Skateboarding
Skating
Ski Jumping
Skimobiling
Sky Diving
Sledding
Snorkeling
Snowmobiling
Snowshoeing
Soccer
Softball
Squash
Stationary Bike
Stretching
Surfing
Swimming
Table Tennis
Tai Chi
Tennis
Track and Field
Trampoline
Trap and Skeet
Unicycling
Volleyball
Walking
Wallyball
Water Aerobics
Water Jogging
Water Polo
Water Skiing
Weight Training
Whitewater Rafting
Wrestling
Yoga

Commit to be fit.
—Author Unknown

Journal Entries

Alisa: *I am taking care of myself physically to look good for Tony, but I also feel good, too.*

Tony: *Back from my bicycling tour. Good to get away and clear my mind. Having not seen Alisa for the last couple of days, I was excited to see her and make love to her.*

Questions

1. It is time to make a positive effort toward improving your physical fitness so that you can enhance your intimacy with your spouse. Haven't exercised in a while and wondering what to do? Look over the activity sheet and pick two or three physical activities you would enjoy.

Husband   Wife

1._____   1._____

2._____   2._____

3._____   3._____

2. What sport did you most enjoy while growing up? Why?

3. What physical features of your spouse do you find attractive?

	Husband	Wife
1.	_____	_____
2.	_____	_____
3.	_____	_____

People who exercise regularly feel better about themselves, feel more sexually desirable and report higher levels of satisfaction.

—Electronic Journal of Human Sexuality

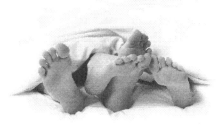

DRESS IT UP PHYSICAL INTIMACY

10

In the previous chapter, we talked about getting physical. In this chapter we take it a step further and talk about the presentation of the package that is YOU.

It should go without saying, but just in case you have forgotten, everyone's body is unique. Clothes that look good on me might not look the same on you, and vice versa. Our physical appearance isn't just our body; it also has to do with how we dress that body and our perception of ourselves. What messages do we send to our spouse via the clothes we choose to wear? Is it: *You are so special to me that I am going to wear my holey sweats and ripped T-shirt?* **OR** *Thank You for making me feel like the most important person! I choose to look, dress and feel my best for you?*

Getting dressed up for your spouse can start with simply getting out of the clothes with the beat-up, had-forever stains and putting on something that makes you feel better about yourself. We are not telling you to go out and spend a fortune on a whole new wardrobe. Rather, invest the time to find a few things that make you feel attractive. Your sense of self will go a long way toward altering the way your spouse sees you.

As you begin to make an effort to improve your physical appearance, take the time to evaluate your body type. We are fans of Stacy London and Clinton Kelly's TLC show, *What Not to Wear*. We love their straightforward, although sometimes tough, approach to helping people get out of the clothing ruts they find themselves in. Their book, *Dress Your Best*, helped both of us to determine what we should be wearing and what we shouldn't. It's time to stop dreaming about the body you wish you had and start dressing the body you do have right now. Try new things, but remember that if you have a few GREAT pieces that make you feel like a million dollars, you are better off than if you had a closet full of clothes that made you feel OK.

Alisa says...

When you were dating, you always wanted to look good, right? What happened to that? Married life doesn't have to be one big fashion show, but making a conscious effort to look nice sends your spouse a signal that you want to recapture an element of courtship in your marriage. You don't have to spend a fortune on clothes or makeup. Just invest some time in your appearance!

Prior to our venture into intimacy, I lived in my mommy uniform: T-shirt and jeans smeared with crumbs, crafts, and whatever else my children happened to have on their hands. There would be times when I would walk by a mirror at the end of the day and barely recognize what I had on. Nice image for my husband, huh?

When you never get out of your mom uniform or your "they're just so comfortable, I don't care what they look like" clothes, it's hard to affect a deep level of intimacy. I began to realize I needed to look and feel better about myself so that I could feel more attractive for and to my husband. Ladies, your husband picked you. He found you to be the most attractive woman he knew. It's time to rediscover that woman.

The show *What Not to Wear* became one of my guilty pleasures a few years ago. After checking out the hosts' book, *Dress Your Best*, I took their advice and shopped for the kinds of pieces best suited to my body. I started wearing makeup (thank you, Carmindy and *The Five Minute Face*). I would don more than the typical T-shirt and jeans. I'd even put on jewelry!

I know what you're thinking – sounds kind of silly for running errands and dropping the kids off at school. But let me tell you what happened. Tony started noticing that I was paying more attention to my appearance. He began to feel more attracted to me

It takes more than just a good-looking body. You've got to have the heart and soul to go with it.

—Epictetus

– and he started stepping up his appearance, too. For the first time in our marriage, he actually went shopping for clothes! Some of you have husbands who like to shop, or have to shop, for suits and other work attire. But my husband is The Dent Dude. He'd spent many years in the paintless dent repair business, where the work required nothing more than a polo shirt and shorts, or jeans if it was cold. So when he started looking more put-together, I was more than a little surprised (as were some of my friends, who had never seen him in anything but shorts).

If this all sounds vain to you, remember this: men are visual creatures. How we look matters to them! Don't break the bank on a new wardrobe, but it doesn't hurt to spend a little of your discretionary income on pieces that make you look and feel great. Husbands, this applies to you, too. Be that handsome man she married. Lose the sweats and put on some slacks when you take her out to dinner. Be that attractive couple that catches everyone's eye.

Tony says...

For the first eleven years of my marriage, I could count on one hand the number of times I dressed up. (That included my wedding day.) I'd never been one who feels a need to wear the most stylish clothes (except during my sophomore year of high school, but that's another story).

In the nearly fifteen years I'd known Alisa, my style hadn't changed much if at all. My closet was filled with shorts, T-shirts, and a jacket for those rare San Diego cold snaps. A button-up shirt was the height of fashion for me. And I wasn't alone; Alisa is the first to admit that style wasn't her priority, either, especially after our two kids came along.

A couple of years after the birth of our second child, Alisa began watching *What Not to Wear*, a makeover show on TLC. After watching for months, she did her own makeover. I was amazed. It got me thinking about my own wardrobe. There's something wrong when most of the clothes in your closet were purchased more than a decade ago. So, just like my wonderful wife, I began to make some changes. It's interesting how something external can make a difference on the inside, too. We acquired new self-images, and we did it all on a budget.

The best part is when Alisa and I go out on our date nights. The looks she gives me let me know I have made another successful step in enhancing our intimacy.

Journal Entries

Alisa: *It amazes me to see how the little changes make such a difference in how I feel about myself and how others see me. I put on some jewelry and makeup today, and a complete stranger not only held open the door for me, but did a double take. Talk about an ego boost!*

Tony: *I went to Kohl's today and bought some nice clothes for the first time in years. It's going to be fun to dress up for Alisa on our next Date Night.*

A smile is an inexpensive way to improve your looks.

—Charles Gordy

Questions

1. What would you like to see your mate wear on your next Date Night?

2. What has been in the closet (or dresser) way too long? This would be a great time to go through your closet and free up some space getting rid of clothes that are out of style, don't fit, don't flatter, etc. Find an organization to donate to and experience the freedom of a clean closet and the sense of giving.

3. Personal Reflection: When I wear _____, I feel attractive.

The best color in the whole world is the one that looks good on you!

—Coco Chanel

RADIO SHACK TO LOVE SHACK
PHYSICAL INTIMACY

11

Making improvements on the appearance of other things in your life can go a long way toward picking up the romance in your marriage, too.

When you think of your bedroom, do you think *sanctuary*? Or do you think *super-messy*? Is it a place where the two of you can come to reconnect, or is it a place where the kids' toys compete with the TV and the laundry for floor space? Would you rather sleep in your own room or go to a hotel? After years of working on this, I finally heard Tony say he would rather sleep in our own room because of the comfort and luxury it now provides. That's not to say that we haven't, or don't, struggle with the mess in our room. However, we have become more conscious of making it a place of retreat, a place to recharge.

Where should you start?

Is the trash out of your room?

Is the clutter gone?

Donate the clothes that don't fit, the books you don't want, and any other stuff that interferes with the mood you are trying to set. And remember, if there's something you haven't worn for more than 6 to 12 months (allowing for seasonal wardrobes), get rid of it!

Move the computers, televisions and cell phones out of your bedroom. I know this one is going to meet with a lot of resistance, but I strongly suggest you try it.

Take the time to discuss what a sanctuary means to the two of you, and begin setting the mood.

Think about your bedding. What size bed do you find most comfortable? Spend a little extra to get really nice sheets. After all, you spend hours on them every night.

Look at the lighting in your room. Can you dim the lights? Are there places for candles? Pillows? Do you have music? Do you like certain scents? If so, the bedroom is definitely the place for a little aromatherapy.

Alisa says...

Does your bedroom look more like a Radio Shack® than a love shack? Are there piles of books or papers cluttering up your space? Are there dishes that belong in the kitchen or clothes that should be put away? That doesn't seem especially conducive to intimacy, does it? Your bedroom should be your love nest, inviting and nurturing.

Take a good look at your bedroom. Yes, right now. Put down the book and take a few minutes to really evaluate your room. If you're like most people, it's full of *things:* clothes on the floor, nightstands littered with the contents of emptied pockets and purses, and an array of televisions and entertainment systems.

My portion of this chapter could be called *Confessions of a Messy Spouse.* I drop my clothes on the floor. I don't always stack my books neatly on the nightstand. Some days, I don't make the bed. And you know what? When I let those things happen, our bedroom feels like just another room in our house. I don't like that. I want it to feel like our private oasis.

For many people, it's the high-tech stuff that's the problem. We're pretty good about this; we have never had a TV in our room (though I admit that the laptop sometimes makes it in). I know some of you reading this will find that strange, but the reality is that televisions and computers in the bedroom can be detrimental to your relationship. Why? Because they're distractions. How often do you start watching TV or go online to check your email and completely zone out?

The ability to simplify means to eliminate the unnecessary so that the necessary may speak.

—Hans Hofmann

Many of us spend all day at the computer. When we're home, shouldn't we be giving our spouse the time and attention he or she deserves? If you're not convinced, consider this: Research shows that basking in the glow of the TV or computer screen for as little as one hour before bedtime is enough to upset your circadian rhythm, delaying sleep – and it may increase risk of disease, too. Need another reason to move the tube? A new study of 523 couples found that a TV in the bedroom decreases sexual desire by about 50%." (Source: *www.prevention.com*)

On to room décor: remember, you are creating a sanctuary, a retreat. Find artwork that compliments your sense of style and your bedroom mood. Try different combinations of colors to create an atmosphere. Need help with this? Check out design magazines from the library or think about your favorite hotel rooms. These are great places to get ideas on how to make your bedroom the perfect escape.

I'm a scrapbooker and love tons of photos, but not in the bedroom. Do you really want to roll over and see a picture of Great-Grandma when you're making a move on your spouse? Extended family and friends are important, but consider keeping them off your nightstand and dresser. We recently discussed this topic in a small group we lead, and the following week one couple decreed it one of the best things they had done to enhance their intimacy:

> *"We hadn't ever really thought about the fact that there were pictures of the family all over our dresser. Last week, we went home and realized there were lots of people in the pictures who didn't really belong there. We have since moved the pictures, and it has dramatically changed the feel of our bedroom."* —M.C.

This couple subsequently moved to a new home, and the wife told me they weren't tempted to put the extended family back on the dresser:

> *"You'll be happy to know that there is not one single family picture in the bedroom. No in-laws or cousins or uncles... only pictures of us. Wedding pictures that were never out before are now displayed prominently!"* —M.C.

Another hint to make your bedroom a more intimate spot: Invest in it. For most couples, the bedroom is the only place where they make love. Yet it's neglected, since not many people see it. You don't have to go overboard, but think about spending some money on good linens, installing dimmer switches, adding wall sconces – anything that will help inspire romance in your relationship.

Tony says...

Ah, the bedroom. It's a place where I can relax and let the outside world fade away. It's extraordinarily inviting, with walls painted in shades that calm and soothe the soul, sheer drapes, and lighting that can be dimmed at the touch of a button. It's a refreshing and recharging room, where Alisa and I talk, dream, and make love.

Before we had children, we had the whole house to ourselves. We could do what we wanted, where we wanted, any time of day. After kids, I realized we needed a place we could truly call our own. Transforming our room didn't happen overnight. It took time and effort, but it was well worth it when we saw the effect it had on our mood and libido.

Is your bedroom stacked high with laundry? Magazines lying around? Computer screen serving as a nightlight? If so, it's time for a change. And men, don't leave this up to your wives. Help put the laundry away, make the bed, and take the time to hook up your home office elsewhere. Those little steps pay great dividends when it comes to building intimacy.

Journal Entries

Alisa: *How different intimacy is now that we have made our bedroom a sanctuary. Plush sheets, candlelight sconces, soothing colors. I love coming into this room to be with Tony.*

Tony: *Candles and vanilla are what I walked into when I entered our room this evening. Alisa looked beautiful in her sexy negligee. It was a change to be sought after. I need to thank Alisa with a little something special for all she is doing to make this time together possible.*

Good lighting is the key to creating a cozy feel in your bedroom. You should have the ability to lower the lights so they are dim and romantic...

—Hans Hofmann

Questions

1. What changes could you make to your bedroom to make it a Love Shack?

2. What sets the mood for you? Lighting, Aromatherapy, Music, etc.

3. What one electronic item needs to get out of your bedroom?

Be calm, let your mind relax, and get inspired... so you can create your own sanctuary.

—www.wholeliving.com

A LITTLE ROMANCE
PHYSICAL
INTIMACY

12

Romance is not just Valentine's Day gifts or some extravagant evening. While no one complains about the big romantic events, the magic lies in doing the little things that say "I love you" or "I want to make things easier for you": remembering her birthday, making his favorite dinner, picking out the flowers she loves, or wearing the dress he loves to see you in.

Being romantic varies widely from couple to couple, but at its core, romance involves doing things to express affection for your spouse in meaningful yet unexpected ways. A true act of romance requires creativity, sincerity and selfless giving, inspired by love. Feeling affection for your spouse might be easy; translating it into romance might not. While there are millions of romantic ideas in books and movies and on the Internet, true romance comes from within you.

Think outside the box to get in touch with your inner romantic.

1. Give a compliment when it's least expected. When was the last time you mentioned how beautiful your wife looks? How about how well your husband barbecued dinner?

2. Spend time together. This isn't just time at home doing the chores, but quality time; for example, when the two of you are engaged

in conversation, playing a board game, or walking along the beach. Where can the two of you spend meaningful time together?

3. Do a little something that says I Love You. If the urge strikes you, go for it. It doesn't have to be extravagant: a single flower, a home-made card, bringing home your spouse's favorite ice cream or something small that shows your love. What can you do to say "I Love You" throughout the year?

4. Let me serve you. Most everyone likes to be served, but it is when we serve our spouses with a loving heart that we are transformed, and our marriages as well. Choose to do her household chores, take out the garbage for him, make dinner for her or get his car washed. Serving each other changes the outlook for both of us. What can you do to serve your spouse?

5. Share the touches that make a difference. These are non-sexual touches that bring you closer together. A hug, a kiss, holding hands, doing anything in which you share physical touch just to say "I love you" or "You are important to me." What touches will spark excitement in your marriage?

What can you do today that says "I love you"?

Alisa says...

Remember when you were dating? Putting a little effort into setting the mood didn't seem like too much trouble. Investing some time and thought into making your marriage more romantic will go a long way toward enhancing intimacy.

During those courting days, he would hand you flowers when you opened the door. You had candles lit, and music playing in the background. You wore that dress he loved, and he had on your favorite cologne.

Now fast-forward a few years.

Spending money on flowers? Not when you have bills to pay. You don't light candles out of fear that the kids will set the house on fire. The only music you hear is the Backyardigans© theme song. You're lucky if you even remember what outfit he likes on you. And cologne… does he even own any?

Life certainly evolves after you get married, but that doesn't mean romance has to end. In fact – and it took us a long time to realize this – romance is all the more important

The word 'romance,' according to the dictionary, means excitement, adventure, and something extremely real. Romance should last a lifetime.

—Billy Graham

once mortgages, kids, and other obligations enter the picture. It helps you remember that you chose each other. Courting your spouse is critical to the success of your marriage. Injecting some much-needed romance into your relationship keeps it strong enough to weather life's ups and downs.

Admittedly, there are days when you just aren't in the mood to be romantic. But sometimes you need to put aside your own feelings to give that gift to your spouse. Choosing to be selfless is a conscious act of love that your husband or wife won't soon forget. We live in a selfish society, one that often encourages us to prioritize our own wants and desires. Taking time for acts of romance shows that we are capable of placing our spouse's needs above our own.

Romantic gestures don't have to be expensive, complicated, or pre-planned. You could text a loving message to your spouse in the middle of the day, pick up dinner, clean the house, or give your husband or wife a long hug – anything that lets your spouse know you care.

The best part of random acts of romance is that you get romanced back! Yes, romance engenders more romance, creating a cycle of love that is certain to create a deeper level of intimacy in your marriage. Take the time to woo your spouse. There was a time when it was your highest priority. Make it a priority again

Tony says...

We are so busy these days that we forget how important it is to romance our spouse. I'm the first to admit that I have trouble in this area. I get so caught up in the big things happening around me that I forget about the little things that can make such a big difference in my marriage – things like candles, flowers, and a card "just because."

When we were dating, I made it a point to not just tell Alisa I loved her – I showed her. But that waned over the years. After all, we were already married. What would be the point of courting her? Here's the point: when I wasn't making the effort, our marriage began to lack real sexual intimacy. As men, we need to realize that our wives like us to notice and appreciate them for everything they do for us. (And believe me, they do more than we realize.) Making life better in the bedroom requires romantic gestures outside the bedroom.

So how do you reignite romance? Take a trip down memory lane. What are some of the special things you did for your spouse before you got married? Try doing some of those things again. Need some ideas? Talk to your spouse about what would make him or her feel loved. One of my favorite ways to stimulate romance is lighting candles in our room. It's such a simple way to create a romantic atmosphere. Gestures like that have added a real spark to our intimacy. Give it a try, and be prepared to enjoy a better sex life and a better marriage.

Journal Entries

Alisa: *Both home during the day – nooner.*

Tony: *Emailed an "I Love You" card to Alisa this morning.*

All I really, really want our love to do is to bring out the best in me and in you too.

—Joni Mitchell

Questions

1. When you were courting, what did you to do wow each other?

2. What three things can you do or say to set the mood?

Husband	Wife
1._____	1._____
2._____	2._____
3._____	3._____

3. Where in everyday activities do you see your spouse's love?

You don't love someone for their looks, or their clothes, or for their fancy car, but because they sing a song only you can hear.

—Anonymous

CHANGE OF SCENERY
PHYSICAL INTIMACY

13

Do you remember the excitement you would experience as a child, getting ready to go someplace you hadn't been before or trying something new? How you would wake up early, filled with anticipation?

As we grow up, with all of our responsibilities and obligations, we seem to lose sight of how much we enjoy trying new things. We have to remind ourselves that even though it's easier to maintain existing routines, a change in scenery really does bring the spark back into our relationships.

Why is this so important? Because routine can easily lead to boredom, especially in your sex life. There's nothing wrong with the "tried and true," but why not shake things up a bit? Bring the excitement and anticipation back into your relationship by trying something new – both in and out of the bedroom.

It doesn't take much to add a little spice to your relationship. Everything from a new hairstyle to a new restaurant to having sex in another room of the house can refresh you mentally and physically. Remind yourself that breaking out of the boredom is worth the effort.

Alisa says...

Same place, same time, every time? To recharge your sex life, get out of your bedroom! Variety is good.

If you have been married for any length of time, your sex life probably seems something like this: TUNE IN NEXT WEEK, SAME BAT-TIME, SAME BAT-CHANNEL. (If you don't get that, you are probably younger than us.)

One couple Tony and I know used to consider Saturday night "sex night." She would shave her legs, he would take her to dinner, and then they would come home and have sex. Not a lot of anticipation or excitement; they were just going through the motions of lovemaking… Thank you very much, and see you next week.

Remember the days when you would try out different rooms in the house, or even (gasp) make love somewhere else? You had sex when you felt like it, not just when you were crawling into bed at night. So what happened? Life happened! But once Tony and I began making an effort to shake things up, intimacy became exciting again.

It isn't difficult to recapture an element of the unexpected in your sex life. You might venture into other rooms of your house (provided the kids aren't around); tryst at a hotel; enjoy a romantic night in a tent on a camping trip; even try a hot night in the car.

Please understand, we're not advocating indecent exposure. But I experienced making love in the car for the first time on my 30th birthday, and I must tell you that it was very exciting – if for no other reason than the thought that we could be caught! Not that it would have mattered – two consenting, married (to each other) adults caught making love in a car in a deserted area isn't going to make the cover of Cosmo unless one of them is a celebrity. But it went a long way toward spicing up our love life.

And here's a novel idea: sex doesn't have to be restricted to the nighttime hours. Wake up early and have great sex to start your day, or meet each other for lunch and a little extra.

Doing something different doesn't apply only to sex. Have your conversations somewhere other than in bed. Tony and I connect while lying on a blanket in the living room, during a walk along the beach, or on a hike.

You can't beat sex outdoors, but there are not many places I haven't done it. Forests, barns, in swimming pool changing rooms, on top of hills, you name it.

—Katie Price

Change is good. Living in such a busy society makes it easy to fall into boring routines. I know, because we've done it. Tony and I are now training ourselves to do different things. We are trying new activities from our Top 10 List, going to different restaurants, and finding ways to make our sex life more interesting. By breaking the routine, we keep our relationship fresh and exciting.

Tony says...

Sex is supposed to be an awesome experience. That's what you hear, but after many years with Alisa I must admit that intimacy had lost its sheen. When we did make love, we did it the same way each and every time. I initiated things and hoped she would respond. Sometimes she did, and sometimes she didn't. Can anyone feel my pain here?

It became a particular passion of mine (no pun intended) to exact some change in this area of our life. You too can make change happen. In order to do that, though, someone in the marriage will have to bring the issue up to the other person. While I was a little nervous about discussing this with Alisa, it was well worth it. We began to open up to each other about different sexual positions, places to make love, and our intimate desires.

This is not to say that it's an amorous adventure every time. We still have our routines, but now we are open and willing to interject a change of scenery when needed.

Journal Entries

Alisa: *I am letting down some of my stuffiness, getting out of the box, trying new positions and new places—even the car! What a rush to be 34 years old, having sex in the car on a deserted road in a new housing development! It totally felt like we were teenagers. I kept waiting for a police officer to knock on the window.*

Tony: *Took a hike with Alisa, with the plan that we would make love at the top of the mountain. Awesome to be out in nature enjoying God's glory and my wife.*

Questions

1. In what one place, inside or outside your home, would you like to make love?

2. Would you rather make love in the back seat of your car or on the top of a mountain? Why?

3. Is there a sexual position or physical touch you would like to explore?

Change is the essence of life. Be willing to surrender what you are for what you could become.

—Anonymous

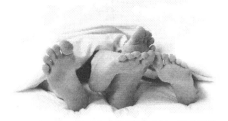

PRAYER WORKS SPIRITUAL INTIMACY

14

Have you ever invited God into your bedroom?

I'm not just talking about the "down on your knees by the side of the bed prayer time," but rather, "God, this is our bedroom, where we are most intimate, and we want you to be a part of this place and our relationship." So often, we give lip service to the idea that we pray for all things and that God is in control of our lives. But take a minute and think about that. Is He really? Do you want Him to be in bed with you and your spouse? Do you think He belongs there? What would happen if you prayed before, during or after your most intimate experiences with your spouse?

This is going to challenge what a lot of you think. Some may think we are absolutely crazy for bringing this up, but the truth is this: God belongs in your bedroom. Prayer should be a part of your marriage, both in and out of the bedroom.

Our lives are busy. Work, family responsibilities, and other activities preclude quiet time with our spouse and God. We are so weary when we finally fall into bed that we seldom take the time to pray together. We need to nurture the power of prayer in our lives.

The time required does not have to be huge. The commitment to make that time does.

Alisa says...

Sometimes divine intervention is necessary – even in our most intimate moments. Don't be afraid to pray before, during, or after making love. It will work wonders.

Prayer and your sex life are two things most people would never consider speaking of in the same sentence, unless they were praying to have a sex life. But I'm talking about more than that. For one thing, prayer is something you can turn to when you are absolutely, positively not in the mood.

When you don't feel like having sex, do you blow off your spouse? Maybe you take a little longer getting ready for bed, thinking to yourself, 'If I'm lucky, he'll fall asleep and I can just slip into bed." How about the roll over? You roll away from your spouse and face the other way until you hear the snoring, breathing a sigh a relief that you're off the hook for the night. There's also blatant rejection: "I'm not in the mood," or "I'm too tired." Do any of these evasion tactics sound familiar? They do to me. I've either done or said all of these things, and probably many more, over the course of thirteen years of marriage.

When we embarked on our 60 Days of Sex, I had no idea what I was getting myself into. We'd never had that much sex in such a short period of time. The first few weeks were like a honeymoon; we were having fun and discovering passion again. The second half of our experiment was more trying. Tony came down with a virus that led to a migraine, and he was out of commission for a week. Then the kids got sick, and I was completely run down. The idea of being intimate was the furthest thing from my mind, and yet I had made a promise to Tony that we would be intimate every day or night that we could.

I decided to do something I had never done before, not even knowing whether it was okay. I prayed during sex. Not out loud, just in my heart. It was an honest request to God to help me "get in the mood." I didn't know what my prayer would bring. All I knew was that I was at the end of my rope, and I could not honor my commitment to Tony alone.

Was my prayer answered? Yes! My desire for my husband was aroused, and we were able to enjoy another night of intimacy. I find it interesting that I had prayed for so many things in my lifetime, but praying for the intimate relationship I share with my husband had never crossed my mind. It had always seemed like that was one area

"For I know the plans I have for you," declares the LORD, "plans to prosper you and not to harm you, plans to give you hope and a future."

—Jeremiah 29:11 (NIV)

where God shouldn't be. But God formed Adam and Eve and created sex. The Bible even has an entire book (Song of Songs) dedicated to sex. In spite of all that, most of us exclude Him from this portion of our lives.

Back to the story: the sex that night was fantastic. After we finished, I turned to Tony and said something to the effect of, "Honey, I didn't really want to have sex tonight, so I prayed that God would help me get in the mood." Needless to say, Tony was a bit taken aback. I'm not sure whether he was more surprised that I had prayed or that I had told him about it. Either way, he had definitely enjoyed the answer to that prayer!

Prayer has now become a more routine part of our sex life. There are going to be days when being intimate is not high on your list of priorities, but it's something your spouse needs. So don't be afraid to ask for divine intervention!

Tony says...

You did what?

That was my first thought as I looked at Alisa after she told me that she had begun praying during foreplay. Truth be told, it sounded almost inappropriate – but I came to realize that her prayer was an act of obedience to God, and that it had changed the way Alisa viewed her relationship with God and her relationship with me.

Over the years, I'd been one to compartmentalize God, and this was definitely one of those areas where God had not been welcomed. He had access to all the other parts of my life, but in the bedroom while I was making love to Alisa? That was a bit beyond my comprehension. But Alisa was giving God everything she had, lifting up all parts of her life to the Lord. I was struck by her faith in Christ. Alisa's decision to pray and invite God into our most intimate act affected a change in me. I also began praying for our physical intimacy, for my wife, and for our marriage. Everything was now laid out before God, with nothing to hide, nothing to hold back.

Guys, listen to me here. It's not about "Hey God, I need sex tonight." It's about asking God to watch over us in all areas of our lives. Each day, I take some time to pray for Alisa's well being and our well being as a couple. This simple act of obedience has turned a husband who thought sex was all about him into a man who understands that God wants us to use intimacy to build our marital bond.

I urge you to take a leap of faith and begin to unlock the intimacy in your marriage, too. Don't let praying together intimidate you. Start by praying for your spouse and your marriage. You can ask God for wisdom in handling issues in your relationship. If you spouse is "not in the mood," pray that he or she will be receptive to your advances. If *you* are "not in the mood," pray to be receptive to your spouse, for the desire to connect sexually. God knows you more intimately than your spouse ever could, and has great plans for you and your marriage (Jeremiah 29:11). Let Him be a part of your marriage.

Journal Entries

Alisa: *Tony proposed praying together before bed tonight, and we did. Candles and vanilla in the room added some romance. Even a Monday can be extraordinary.*

Tony: *We have wanted to pray together for some time now, and we finally did it tonight. God is in on this with us; though we completely believe this, there are times when we forget. We need to keep Him at the center of our quest. It's tough to pray together, but vital for our marriage. Praying together tonight allowed us to open up and be transparent with each other. All positive.*

Love is an act of faith.

—Erich Fromm

Questions

1. When was the last time you prayed for your spouse? Share what you prayed for.

2. What can you do today that would foster prayer time together?

3. Would you prefer to use a devotional or to free-form your prayers?

God wants to speak to us more than we want to listen. He is a God of love, and love longs to communicate.

—Linda Schubert

Lord, make me grateful for your past blessings,

confident of your future provision,

and at peace with my current circumstances. Amen.

—Author Unknown

RESOURCES

Stripped Down Resources

Visit us online to find additional resources:
www.oneextraordinarymarriage.com/stripped-down-resources

Let's Talk

77 Questions That Get the Conversation Started

201 Great Questions for Married Couples by Jerry Jones

Money Matters

Financial Peace by Dave Ramsey

Eat. Drink. Save Money. http://www.restaurants.com

Pear Budget - http://www.pearbudget.com

What do we do NOW?

Top 10 List Worksheet

Get Physical

Exercise: Key to good sex – CNN.com

American Council of Exercise - http://www.acefitness.org

Dress it Up

What Not to Wear on TLC

Dress Your Best by Clinton Kelly & Stacy London

ONE Community

Join the ONE Community at www.oneextraordinarymarriage.com. You'll connect with other married couples who are having extraordinary marriages, sharing ideas, and doing their part to help others.

ABOUT THE AUTHORS

Tony and Alisa DiLorenzo are authors, speakers, marriage coaches, podcasters, and the founders of ONE. For many years Tony and Alisa have helped couples achieve romance, passion, and intimacy in their marriage. They've been called *Champions of Extraordinary Marriages* and they truly have a passion for their work.

Tony and Alisa created ONE because they felt a need to share what they have learned and discovered throughout their marriage. Helping couples improve their marriages is an honor and a joy for Tony and Alisa. They believe that when marriages are strong, with both spouses connected, couples experience more romance, passion, and ultimately more intimacy.

If you'd like a complimentary 30-minute coaching session with Tony and Alisa, you can make a request at OneExtraordinaryMarriage. com, or call (858)754-9937.

If *Stripped Down* has encouraged you to make intimacy a priority in your marriage and you would like to share it with others, here are some easy ways for you to do so.

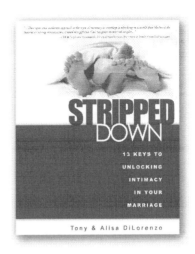

- We blog and podcast on www.OneExtraordinaryMarriage.com every week. Come by, leave a comment and share how *Stripped Down* has made a difference in your marriage.

- To purchase additional copies of *Stripped Down* for your friends, family, and/or small group visit www.OneExtraordinaryMarriage.com.

- Subscribe to our Podcast on iTunes at **ONE Extraordinary Marriage Podcast**.

- Each week we send out to hundreds of subscribers, Marriage Minute Monday, a one minute video tip that you can use in your marriage each week. Go to www.OneExtraordinaryMarriage.com and sign-up.

Join our Facebook Page. Just search **ONE Extraordinary Marriage** and you'll find us. The growing ONE Community is active there and we would love to interact with you there as we pose a weekly question and other fun tidbit about what is happening with ONE.

- We know many of you have blogs, Twitter accounts, Facebook pages, and more. We'd love it if you would write a review of the book along with a link to www.OneExtraordinaryMarriage.com.

- Start a small group at your church or other organization that would benefit and impact your community.

- If you'd like Tony and/or Alisa to appear on your local radio station, podcast, morning TV show, or in print media, send us an e-mail at info@OneExtraordinaryMarriage.com and let us know about it.

- Would you like us to speak to your church, your organization, or conference? If so, send us an email at info@OneExtraordinaryMarriage.com and we'll see what we can arrange.

- Contact us by mail: ONE, PO Box 521, Poway, CA 92074

Since the beginning of ONE, our goal has been to share from our hearts, the hardships and triumphs that we have had in our marriage. We hope that *Stripped Down*, our stories, quotes, and questions will inspire you to want more out of your marriage. Our prayer is that *Stripped Down* has equipped you with the keys that you need to go out and make your marriage extraordinary.

We love you guys!

Tony & Alisa DiLorenzo

Made in the USA
Las Vegas, NV
23 November 2021

35142331R00090